SPIRITUALITY, LEADERSHIP AND SUSTAINING A CARING WORKFORCE

Catholic Social Services Australia acknowledges Traditional Owners of Country throughout Australia and recognises their deep spiritual connection to lands, waters and communities. We pay our respect to Aboriginal and Torres Strait Islander cultures; and to Elders both past and present.

The editors of this book would like to acknowledge the sponsorship and support of the following organisations:

- Catholic Social Services Australia
- Catholic Social Services NSW/ACT
- CatholicCare Greater Melbourne, Geelong, Gippsland
- CatholicCare Tasmania
- Centacare Brisbane
- Centacare Catholic Family Services – Adelaide
- MacKillop Family Services

The views in this book are solely those of the respective contributors and do not claim to represent those of these sponsoring organisations.

SPIRITUALITY, LEADERSHIP AND SUSTAINING A CARING WORKFORCE

Edited by

Brenton Prosser

Foreword – Michael A. Casey

Introduction and Conclusion – Ursula Stephens, CEO
Catholic Social Services Australia

Connor Court Publishing

Published in 2020 by Connor Court Publishing Pty Ltd
Copyright © Catholic Social Services, Australia 2020

All rights reserved. No part of this book may be reproduced or transmitted in any form or by any means, electronic or mechanical, including photocopying, recording or by any information storage and retrieval system, without prior permission in writing from the publisher.

Connor Court Publishing Pty Ltd
PO Box 7257
Redland Bay QLD 4165

sales@connorcourt.com
www.connorcourtpublishing.com.au
Phone 0497 900 685

ISBN: 9781922449078
Front Cover Design: Maria Giordano
Printed in Australia

CONTENTS

FOREWORD – Michael Casey   7

INTRODUCTION – Ursula Stephens   11

ABOUT THE CONTRIBUTING AUTHORS   17

1. WHAT MATTERS MOST – Spirituality, Leadership and Workplace Culture – an Indigenous Perspective – Toni Janke   19

2. FAITH AND WELLBEING – The Hope of Spirituality for Trauma – Fr Frank Brennan SJ AO   31

3. FINDING THE LANGUAGE – Theory and Terms from the Secular Literature – Brenton Prosser   43

4. CARING AT THE COALFACE – Researching Empathetic Labour and Vicarious Resilience – Jonathon Louth   59

5. WHOLE-OF-CULTURE SUPPORT – Introducing the Sanctuary Model for Vicarious Trauma – Robyn Miller   79

6. STAFF AT THE HEART – Practical Strategies for Everyday Spiritual Support – Netty Horton and Nick Collins   95

7. WALKING THE WALK – Leading Catholic Organisations that Foster Connection – Belinda Clarke and Kylie Burgess   103

CONCLUSION   117

FOREWORD

Michael Casey

There are so many good things about our communities and our society – often we take these good things for granted. Amongst all that is good, however, there are Australians who are relegated from society, experiencing life on its margins; suffering neglect, abuse and violence, and significant mental illness - sometimes for a very long time. Fortunately, we have a workforce of dedicated professional people working to support those who have experienced struggle. These dedicated professionals are those in our social services agencies who work to make the lives of individuals and communities better – our society would be significantly diminished without them.

For those fortunate amongst us, we often assume that social services agencies and those working within them will always be there; that there will always be enough funding to deliver supports and services to the vulnerable, and that the devoted social service professionals will always have the capacity, the drive and the energy to undertake their very challenging work. It is one of our many blessings that we can rely on this status quo, but it would be a mistake to do so complacently.

A major reason for avoiding complacency is the toll that caring for people with trauma takes on those who are caring. Helping vulnerable people who have suffered trauma and who have often been left with a legacy of deep mistrust, strong negative emotions, destructive behaviours, and complex and multiple needs, is difficult and demanding work. The emotional and physical resources needed to sustain this work are great, and social service workers cannot do this without being appropriately supported by employers who recognise that working and caring for traumatised people can lead to secondary or vicarious trauma for the carer.

Service providers are increasingly aware of this problem and are developing different ways of responding to it. Social service agencies dedicated to supporting people, must ensure that they are looking after their staff. In addition to this fundamental human dimension, it also makes sense organisationally, to mitigate the risk of losing highly experienced staff and expertise – due to burn-out, stress, compassion fatigue or simple exhaustion.

Catholic social service agencies have particular reasons to be concerned about this problem, their work being founded on deeply held religious convictions about the priority that must be given to the human person created in the image and likeness of God. Failing to care for those undertaking caring work is not an option for any organisation dedicated to caring for others, and significantly not so for Catholic agencies.

Catholic Social Services Australia, the national peak social services body of the Catholic Church, has published this short book of essays *Spirituality, Leadership and Sustaining a Caring Workforce*. These essays provide us with insights into how different agencies undertake to care, support and sustain the spirit of those working on the frontline. Primarily it is a resource for member organisations and their leaders and staff, however, it will also be of interest to those involved in the caring professions more generally.

While the book's main focus is on the experience of workers in social services, the reflections offer understandings on practical initiatives for ensuring that social service workers feel that their work is meaningful to themselves and valued by their employer, that they feel connected to their colleagues and the mission of their organisation, and that they are confident of being supported and helped when they are under pressure. I am sure this will also resonate with those working in fields such as education, health, and pastoral care.

Spirituality, Leadership and Sustaining a Caring Workforce provides some rich reflections on how the expressly religious dimension of the mission of Catholic social services can be a resource for employers and staff in responding to vicarious trauma. Rather than narrowing the readership of the book, this dimension will be of interest well beyond Catholic agencies and other faith-based services. There is growing acknowledgement across religious and secular divides of the importance of different forms of spirituality and mindfulness in helping staff to reduce and work through vicarious trauma. The book summarises some of the research highlighting the importance of religious faith and spirituality, both in sustaining empathy and a commitment to working with traumatised people, and in generating positive feelings among social service professionals about their work, despite the enormous demands and difficulties they face in an ordinary day.

As part of not taking things for granted, attention also needs to be focussed on how those being trained for social service professions are being prepared for encountering trauma and reducing the risk of vicarious trauma for themselves. *Spirituality, Leadership and Sustaining a Caring Workforce* will be useful for this purpose too, serving as an easily accessible resource for educators and students in disciplines such as welfare and social work, education, health care, pastoral services and religious ministry. The experience of people working in social services gathered in this book speaks to carers working in other domains, including in other faith and mission-based services.

Australia is overdue for a serious conversation about the contribution which the caring professions make to our life in common, and about how we recognise, support and value this work.

We rely more than we realise on the commitment that carers make to looking after people who are living with trauma or tragedy, and most of us would be surprised to learn of just how many people – by no means only just from the margins of society – depend on their help to hold things together and keep going. We live in a good country, and the work of these people and the agencies to which they belong helps make it so. If we want to ensure we remain a compassionate nation, we need to do more to care for our social services caring workforce.

Spirituality, Leadership and Sustaining a Caring Workforce is a small but important contribution to addressing a pressing problem. Its purpose is to open up the issue of how spirituality and leadership can build a culture that assists us to sustain and retain a strong dedicated profession of social service workers who are healthy and enriched by their work. Catholic Social Services Australia has done a terrific job in making this resource available, and I hope it will add not only to greater awareness and enhanced responses, but to a larger discussion about the value we place on the role of social services and caring in our country.

Michael A. Casey PhD
Director, PM Glynn Institute
Australian Catholic University

INTRODUCTION

Dr Ursula Stephens

It is critically important that as people working in the social services space we remind ourselves of the extraordinary and complex environment in which we operate. Today we are working in exceptionally challenging times; while drought and bushfire have tested the strength of people, families and their communities, the COVID-19 pandemic is now disrupting lives and livelihoods on a national scale-and testing the resilience of our social and economic structures as never before. This is making extreme demands on our social services work force.

I do believe it is important now, as always, to reflect on our deeper inspiration and common compassion in how we work both as organisations and as individuals. To do so helps us to discover how we might better sustain ourselves to care for each other and for the people we support.

At our Catholic Social Services Member Forum in October 2019, we were privileged to hear from Commissioner Robert Fitzgerald AM, who urged us "to consider **not** how we run our organisations in these complex times, but how disadvantaged Australians live in troubling times. This is what should motivate us in our work", he said. As I reflected on Commissioner Fitzgerald's words, I realized that this is what should be at the core of our thinking, not just now during disasters, but always.

I genuinely believe that we in social services, whether on a leadership team, an expert on the front line or an administrator, are motivated by the notion described by Commissioner Fitzgerald. Commissioner Fitzgerald spoke of three fundamental pillars that are critical to our social service organisations and their success; governance, leadership and culture. In this book we look to these pillars and how they are integral to our ability to build organisational capacity and to retain and sustain a healthy, productive social services workforce and in doing so, give our best to help those experiencing struggle in their lives.

How we motivate ourselves to give our best to those in need is very much drawn from our own individual spirituality. We use this spirituality to guide our vision, insight and energy to be who we are and to do the work we do.

As a network of Catholic social service organisations, we work with those who are vulnerable and living on the margins to help them reclaim their lives. Now more than ever, the services delivered by our network for more than sixty years, is in heightened demand. On a daily basis our network of staff work with struggling communities, broken families, troubled relationships, mental illness, trauma, and substance abuse. This work is demanding, challenging but ultimately it is richly rewarding.

The Gospel teaches us not just to serve the poor and vulnerable, but to serve them in a manner which shows them what God's love is like. If we are burned out, crushed or dispirited, we cannot fulfil God's work. The following collection of essays seeks to inspire, provoke and challenge us in how we imbed our Christian values within our organisations such that they enable us to be refreshed, restored and sustained. In being spiritually refreshed and restored we can be vitalised to sustain our work with our fellow human beings.

Our book opens with a personal and poignant essay from Toni Janke who reflects deeply on her spirituality. Toni is an Aboriginal and Torres Strait Islander woman of Wuthathi and Meriam heritage who was baptised a Catholic. She has rich understandings of spirituality and articulates the notion of leadership that speaks out with patience, gentility, kindness, humility and goodness. As a First Australian Toni gives insight to the need to be the voice to the silent community, coming from a place deep within the heart, of genuine love and concern for the welfare of her mob. Toni speaks of her faith, times of despair and difficulty as well as times of hope, great love and joy; she also gives insight into working in an environment that supports and nourishes her.

The following essay, by Father Frank Brennan SJ AO, Jesuit priest, and professor of law provides a unique perspective of the interface between faith, theory and practice. Profound and sensitive, Father Frank provides insight into the powerful role of spirituality to sustain wellbeing during times of stress, tragedy and trauma. He reflects on the power of lifting our eyes to a horizon of inclusive love, enduring hope and sustaining faith.

Brenton Prosser PhD, provides a range of definitions to inform our reflections, exploring the link between secular literature and the main themes in this collection. Based on Dr Prosser's academic work on a range of conceptual resources, this essay prompts reflection on how we might think and speak about the spiritual in human services work. Chosen for their utility, these perspectives can provide human service leaders with a range of ways to think about the challenge of caring for those who care and are in their care.

Jonathon Louth PhD, provides an overview of the challenges in the service delivery context. Over the last two years, Jonathon has worked with Centacare Catholic Family Services (Adelaide) to explore the impact of compassion fatigue and vicarious resilience on their social service workers. This essay provides an empirical snapshot of the range of challenges faced within a human service agency and will be useful to leaders as they reflect on the conditions within their own organisations.

Continuing the exploration of vicarious trauma, the following essay addresses the question of how leaders might respond to the challenges within the service delivery context. MacKillop Family Services, led by CEO, Dr Robyn Miller, has introduced the Sanctuary Model to respond to issues around vicarious trauma. From frontline to finance, corporate to casuals, Dr Miller tells the story of enhancing support for all through organisational change. Insightful and honest, Dr Miller's narrative about how a social services CEO, immersed in the financial and practical challenges of the role, is persuaded by the need to embrace whole of culture change.

Netty Horton and Nick Collins, from CatholicCare Greater Melbourne, Geelong, Gippsland, provide insight into the management of a social service agency in a reformed social services space. Practically orientated, their account reveals how they retain and manage staff while being true to the principles of Catholic Social Teachings. Personal experience provides the narrative to explore the impact of brutal and harsh stories on the care giver and how as human service professionals, we might find the pathway to restoration and recovery.

In the final contribution, Belinda Clarke and Kylie Burgess from CatholicCare Tasmania give relevance to our Catholic mission and the deeply human connections between those in care, those who provide care and all associated with caring work. This essay delves deep into Catholic tradition to find inspiration for social service leaders and those working on the front line. It provides a deep understanding of the everyday demands of sustaining social service professionals as they encounter situations of despair, trauma and tragedy.

As we confront the pandemic that is COVID-19 we, in the social service sector, continue to work towards best practice workplace management, imbued with the principles of Catholic Social Teaching. The guidance provided in these principles will ultimately always challenge and guide us to care for each other with patience, kindness and compassion.

While I acknowledge that developing a sector that is renowned for a nourished and nurtured workforce is a process of continuous improvement, there is much great work already being done in this space – from sharing of practical ideas and models and strategies to understanding the strength provided by the comfort and capacity for restoration of our own individual spirituality.

By enabling an organisation to develop a culture founded on spirituality, and effective and caring leadership, I believe we are well on the way to building a strong and self-sustaining work force where the risks of staff burnout, compassion fatigue and poor staff retention are significantly reduced.

I hope that you as the reader will be illuminated by the following essays, and that you will see the great work that is happening in our social service organisations. I am optimistic you will learn from personal accounts and reflections and be inspired to continue to build your organisation and ultimately our sector.

May our sector be recognised for its caring and compassion, and for its strong and resilient workforce. And I hope this book of essays will provide opportunities for personal reflection and growth. To stimulate the conversations that may emerge from reading this collection, we have provided some questions, which may be used individually or in group discussion.

Dr Ursula Stephens
CEO Catholic Social Services

ABOUT THE CONTRIBUTING AUTHORS

Toni Janke is a Wuthathi and Meriam woman and holds graduate and post-graduate qualifications in law, ministry, and theology. Ms Janke is a singer/songwriter and writes prayers, poetry and mediations. She is the Coordinator of Indigenous Services, Centacare Family & Relationship Services, Brisbane. Ms Janke is a strong advocate for social justice, reconciliation and unity between Indigenous and non-Indigenous people.

Father Frank Brennan SJ AO, is a Jesuit priest, lawyer, professor and human rights activist, and is well known for his decades-long work as an advocate in the areas of law, social justice, refugee and human rights protection, and Aboriginal reconciliation. Fr Frank is currently the rector at Newman College Melbourne, and previous CEO Catholic Social Services Australia.

Professor Brenton Prosser PhD is Director of the National Social and Economic Modelling Centre in Canberra. A former teacher, teacher educator and health researcher, he has published widely on the human service professions. Professor Prosser was director of research at Catholic Social Services Australia from 2018 to 2020.

Jonathon Louth PhD is a research fellow at the UniSA Australian Alliance for Social Enterprise. He has worked across government, the community sector and academia both in Australia and the United Kingdom. Dr Louth has previously worked as an advisor for the South Australian Government.

Robyn Miller PhD is the CEO of MacKillop Family Services, one of the largest providers of specialist services to vulnerable and disadvantaged children, young people and their families in Australia. Dr Miller was previously the Chief Practitioner within the Department of Human Services in Victoria.

Nick Collins is the Executive Manager of Operations at CatholicCare Greater Melbourne, Geelong, Gippsland. He is a Psychologist with extensive experience in providing and managing social and community services over 25 years. Nick Collins has a Masters in Counselling Psychology and a diploma in impact leadership.

Netty Horton is Chief Executive Officer, CatholicCare Greater Melbourne, Geelong, and Gippsland. She has held a number of leadership and executive roles demonstrating her long-term commitment to working with the vulnerable and disadvantage. Netty Horton is a Churchill Fellow and has a Master in Public Policy.

Kylie Burgess is Centacare Evolve Housing's Manager of Community Wellbeing in Hobart. She has worked in Catholic Social Services for more than seven years, including as Social Impact Designer with CatholicCare Tasmania and Director of Mission with Catholic Social Services Australia.

Belinda Clarke is current and founding Director of the Social Impact Program with CatholicCare Tasmania. Belinda Clarke has executive and leadership experience across healthcare, community, social services, education, and business sectors she holds a Master in Education and Leadership.

1

WHAT MATTERS MOST
Spirituality, Leadership and Workplace Culture an Indigenous Perspective

Toni Janke

My family originally come from Cape York and the Torres Strait. I identify as an Aboriginal and Torres Strait Islander woman of Wuthathi and Meriam heritage. I was baptised as a Catholic at St Rita's Catholic Church in Babinda in October 1965. I attended Catholic primary and secondary schools in Cairns and later Canberra where I learned about God, Jesus, Mary and Joseph, Gospel values and most importantly, how different I appeared (even as a young child) to be from everyone else around me.

I learned about racism, shame, injustice and inequality when I was growing up. But I also learned about friendship, determination, courage, independence and our capacity to overcome challenges. I learned about the importance of family - social and cultural connection and that unbreakable bond that is grounded in my identity and sense of belonging no matter where I go or what I do.

I studied and lived in Sydney, NSW, Brisbane and the Gold Coast. I graduated from the University of New South Wales in 1989 as one of the youngest Indigenous graduates at the time with a Bachelor of Arts/Law. I later completed post-graduate studies at the Australian Catholic University. I have been privileged to have worked in Aboriginal and Torres Strait Islander affairs for the past three decades, at various levels, in community organisations, non-government agencies as well as for State and Federal Government agencies.

I have served on many boards and committees working with other Aboriginal and Torres Strait Islander colleagues, many with whom I have developed life-long friendships. I have also had a successful career as a professional singer/songwriter, working in the media and arts. I have two grown up daughters, who are by far my greatest achievement.

I now work for Centacare Family and Relationship Services in Archdiocese of Brisbane as the Coordinator of Indigenous Services. Centacare is a large non-government organisation providing frontline services to vulnerable families across south-east Queensland. We are the social justice arm of the Catholic Church in Brisbane - the hands and feet of Christ working with people from all walks of life, mostly vulnerable families as they try to navigate fractured systems.

From this standpoint, I am humbled to be asked to contribute to this book. Many others are much more qualified than I am to do so, and I am sure they would be able to write far more eloquently than I can and with greater experience as well. However, I would simply like to share my personal and professional insight and experience to contribute what I have learned and observed about spirituality, leadership and workplace culture from both a faith-based organisational lens and an Indigenous perspective.

I do not in any way purport to speak on behalf of anyone else - black or white, male, female or other. Nor do I speak on behalf of any particular faith tradition. I simply want to contribute my own reflective experience here that it might add some value.

I acknowledge that I have an important role and contribution to make to my community and my workplace, although I am not an

Elder, nor do I have any special wisdom or expertise. I am just one of many. Yet in my role, I am required to speak out about issues that relate to my community, families and the people that I work for and with every day. It is never purely about who we are as individuals, but rather what we can do in our positions, to further advocate for social justice and freedom for others.

I am also mindful and conscious of the need to consistently observe cultural protocols and to acknowledge and respect others as appropriate. Indeed, protocols are more important than people and titles, as is ceremony and ritual. In the same way, time and money are not the most important considerations. What is important and always has been is the people. We should never lose sight of who we are working for, just as it is equally important to ensure that the right people are at the table, participating in the process, which is also usually more important than any outcome of itself.

I believe these are fundamental starting points of good leadership irrespective of who we are or where we come from. This essay explores some of the attributes and similarities between Indigenous and non-Indigenous leadership as it applies to those of us working within a faith-based organisational context. I also look at some of the challenges that we face on a day to day basis as leaders.

Several scholars, Indigenous and non-Indigenous have identified fundamental differences between white Eurocentric models of leadership and Indigenous leadership.[1] Indigenous leadership is essentially viewed as a 'multi-faceted and complex phenomenon that offers a rich arena for challenging existing leadership paradigms and advancing extant leadership theories'.[2] It is often spoken about in terms

---

1   Fraser T, Kenny C. Living Indigenous Leadership: Native Narratives on Building Strong Communities. University of British Columbia Press; 2012.
2   Picard M, McCulloch A, Adams R, Ahlberg A, Aitchson C, Albertyn R et al. Proceedings of the 12th biennial Quality in Postgraduate Research (QPR) conference, Adelaide, South Australia April 20-22, 2016.

of solidarity, self-determination and our capacity to communicate effectively with others and 'walk between two worlds'.³ However, it is (as is all authentic leadership), relational above all else.⁴

As Indigenous people, we often don't get to choose whether we speak up or not. We do so because we must and because of the position we are placed in. It is often more of an obligation or responsibility but is also both a gift and privilege.⁵ To decline to speak up is generally not an option. It is much like a deep force within us that calls us towards something for which we are destined to do, not just because of the position we hold, but paradoxically because of who we are and where we come from. I have experienced this often and at many points in my life. I know it as the beckoning of my ancestors – so strong in its pull that we cannot but comply. I also know it as God or the Holy Spirit, working in and through me, constantly prompting me, shaping, leading and guiding me.⁶

As frontline workers in the community sector, we encounter those who are marginalised and vulnerable every day. By virtue of our privileged position, we have an increasing responsibility to act for justice, to advocate, to speak out and stand up for those who are often voiceless. Never before in our history have we seen such stark social, economic, cultural and political challenges,⁷ yet still so much more needs to be done to really address the heart of the many complex and nuanced issues.

---

3   Kenny & Kenny, ibid, p. 6
4   Pless, N. & Maak, T. Responsible Leadership. Dordrecht: Springer Netherlands; 2012.
5   7. Young A. Elders' teachings on indigenous leadership. [Vancouver, B.C.]: University of British Columbia; 2006.
6   1 Corinthians 2:4-5
7   Escobar A. Beyond the Third World: imperial globality, global coloniality and anti-globalisation social movements [Internet]. Taylor & Francis. 2020 [cited 26 May 2020]. Available from: https://doi.org/10.1080/0143659042000185417

Why is it that so many of our brothers and sisters still suffer in a country and society where suffering should have been eradicated long ago? Our prisons are over-crowded. Our health, welfare and criminal justice systems perpetuate harm and suffering. Our kids are being removed from their families. Mental health, drug and alcohol addiction, unemployment, domestic and family violence, child abuse and neglect, youth suicide, homelessness, trauma and poverty[8]– all of these factors impact on our families every day in a world driven by consumerism and individualism that ironically is supposed to have made us more socially connected, technologically savvy, sophisticated and more globally aware and responsive.

Successive governments have tried to find solutions but I believe that economic and/or political solutions are not by themselves sufficient. Public awareness and education is also, sadly not enough. The constant cry for greater social and cultural inclusion at all levels indicates that there is still so much work for all of us to do. Yet, those of us in faith-based organisations who deliver services to those in need, know that what sustains and nourishes us (despite the many challenges and complexities of our day-to-day work) comes from the spiritual domain - not people, not governments, bureaucracies or systems. Our faith, spirituality and shared values such as empathy, compassion, dignity and respect are distinguishing features that sustain us in contemporary leadership.[9]

We are created as human beings, yet we are social, cultural and

---

8   Close the Gap Report 2020 [Internet]. Lowitja.org.au. 2020 [cited 26 May 2020]. Available from:
https://www.lowitja.org.au/page/services/resources/Cultural-and-social-determinants/culture-for-health-and-wellbeing/close-the-gap-report-2020
https://humanrights.gov.au/our-work/aboriginal-and-torres-strait-islander-social-justice/publications/close-gap-2020

9   Does Faith Matter [Internet]. Www3.weforum.org. 2020 [cited 26 May 2020]. Available from: http://www3.weforum.org/docs/GAC/2014/WEF_GAC_RoleFaith_DoesFaithMatter_Report_2014.pdf

spiritual beings – human and divine. As co-creators with God, most of us are called to this line of work with a profound urge to serve others.[10] We acknowledge the importance of healing and restoring those among us who are hurting or traumatised, not because we are particularly virtuous but because it is the right thing to do. We play our part, irrespective of who we are, what we believe, where we come from or what stage of the journey we ourselves may be at.

Neither do we pontificate about values and principles. We must live and practice them daily in the workplace. In this way, we continually reassess our priorities to remind us what is fundamentally important and essential, for our collective survival and the common good of all. Shared decision-making through open and transparent leadership is vital.[11] This is even more evident in the not for profit sector where one of our biggest challenges is where and how to allocate limited resources – time and money.

Another significant challenge that I believe we face today as workers in the social justice area, is to speak out about our faith in a secular world that is extremely angry and sceptical, and perhaps justifiably so. As faith-based organisations, we have to clean up the horrendous wrongs of the past by openly acknowledging the deep pain and sorrow caused to others[12]. This is not an easy task. However, we must move forward walking hand in hand with God and each other in all our diversity and difference. There is no other real option.

Neither is it about professing a simplistic, blind faith that shirks responsibility or accountability. We must always look deeper beyond our limited humanity, our frailty and fallibility - towards our unfailing

---

10 Hyejung J. Human Beings as Co-Creators with God: The Search for Workers' Dignity in Capitalist Society. Asian Journal of Religion and Society. 2018; 6(2).

11 Fletcher J. Disappearing Acts. Cambridge: MIT Press; 2015.

12 King F. Can the Catholic Church clean up her own mess? [Internet]. Frank King's Blog. 2018 [cited 26 May 2020]. Available from: https://frankking.net/2018/09/can-the-catholic-church-clean-up-her-mess/

will to serve God and others more than anything else, especially in troubled times.[13]

In this respect, authentic leadership is about taking action by living out our values and speaking up respectfully and boldly for what we believe to be right.[14] Do we put our values into actual practice every day as part of our workplace culture? It is not about being holier than thou or finger-pointing. Authentic leadership is never about being authoritative, judgemental or arrogant. Nor do we stand over others or compare ourselves to them.

As an Indigenous woman, authentic leadership is about speaking out patiently and gently with kindness, humility and goodness - in a language that is non-threatening so others may learn and gain a better understanding of our plight. We must be strong and blatantly honest, yet calm and persistent in reminding others (and ourselves) about the importance of both mutual action and accountability. Creativity and resourcefulness are key attributes as are self-care, ongoing reflective practice and the need for collegial support. But we can only do so much. In faith-based organisations, we know and accept that God is in charge as the source of hope for all, even when life may seem hopeless.

Many times we must also be the voice of our silent community - our brothers and sisters, aunties and uncles, our Elders – for anyone who is still suffering. We come from a place deep within the heart; of genuine love and concern for the welfare of all our mob. We have been brought up in our families, our communities and our culture to respect everyone and to always look out for those less fortunate than us while at the same time, never forgetting who we are and where

---

13 Goudzwaard B, Vennen M, Van Heemst D. Hope in troubled times. Baker Academic; 2007.
14 Massaro T. Mercy in Action: The Social Teachings of Pope Francis. Rowman & Littlefield Publishers; 2018.

we come from. Authentic Indigenous leadership is not violent or aggressive. It does not seek to attack others. It does not engage in lateral violence. It is always truthful, sincere, forgiving, tolerant and often humorous, particularly in the face of hardship, despair and suffering.

One of the most valuable learnings I have observed from those who have gone before me as strong Indigenous leaders and role models is the constant need to advocate for others, for future generations whilst remaining ever-mindful of our sacred connection to, and relationship with place – to Country, the land, the sea, rivers and mountains, the sun, moon, sky and all the stars, animals, birds, totems – the entire natural world, the universe and cosmos - past, present and future.[15]

As an Aboriginal and Torres Strait Islander Catholic woman, I am proud of who I am although I am also deeply ashamed of the treatment that many of our people have endured as the direct result of previous grave historical injustices. I am embarrassed about how slow the wheels of change turn in institutions and bureaucracies while people are still hurting and dying at appalling rates. Yet, my faith and hope is greater.

I remember wondering as a small child why I was black, why I was different. Why did God make me the way I am? I've never really had a straight answer from God to any of these questions, but my father's attempt to console me as a young child comes close. He would often say to me, 'Look in the mirror. You will always be black but you can achieve anything you set your mind to'.

We grow up fast because of what we have seen, how we have been treated or what we have experienced in our lives - injustice, hardship, unfairness, racism, sexism and discrimination. It's our first-hand bitter experiences that shape how we interpret the world. We often know

---

15 Hall, G., Hendriks, J., & Panikkar, R. Dreaming a new earth. Preston, Vic.: Mosaic Press; 2012.

how others feel and what they are going through. It is this relational pain and sadness of our own lived experience that often says 'I sees the injustice here. Why are we not doing something about it?' You get to a point where you have to speak up, because not to do so goes against every grain in your body. It's like our ancestors or Elders are continually urging us on, saying 'Go on then bub. Step up, you tell them'.

Certainly, I have had constant reassurance and love from God, who also tells me that He loves me regardless, and whilst I may never understand many things, I can absolutely trust in His vision and plan for us all. This has been the one consistent premise of my faith, in times of despair and difficulty as well as in times of hope, great love and joy; when I have become so disheartened that I wanted to walk away and quit and when I have found immense happiness in service and giving to others. Working in an environment that supports and nourishes me is a blessing.

However, no matter where I have worked, the end goal has always been the same – how best to serve the needs of Aboriginal and Torres Strait Islander people either on the frontline, day to day or by working in policy development and leadership. We can achieve many things through mutual understanding and respect. We should never underestimate the power of relational flexibility and tolerance as mechanisms for radical change, forgiveness and love.

In my experience the best leaders are often those who say or do the least. They pave the way for others and lovingly encourage everyone to have their say or play their part; they draw out the gifts and talents of those around them. They don't seek to be better than. They are usually genuinely embarrassed by praise or big-noting. They speak from the heart and are skilfully able to identify what is essential and non-essential. We have been reminded of this during the recent COVID 19 pandemic. Have we become more acutely aware of the stark nature of chronic disadvantage, systemic poverty and vulnerability? How does this apply to us in an Australian context as well as a global context? What is really important in our everyday work? What exactly are our priorities?

And yet, social justice should never be about competing priorities but respectfully acknowledging the rights of all people. Let us resist the temptation to become apathetic in a take-a-ticket-and-wait-in-the-queue approach to social services, only to find that by the time our turn comes around, governments have changed, rules are different, there's a new system now and we must start again at the bottom of the heap. Sorrow is shallow when our people are still dying.

Of course, this is the environment we work in every day as frontline workers. It is complex, challenging and baffling. Words like poverty, homelessness, unemployment, incarceration, addiction, child protection, suicide and so on cease to have any real meaning or emotion because they are frequently spoken of and often seen as big problems without any real or lasting solutions. But we have to move from that terrible place of fear to a place of faith - that all is not completely hopeless, even though we must accept the practical reality that many challenges and injustices take a long time to be rectified.

Still we keep moving forward. We challenge, we lobby, we advocate, we cry, but we keep praying. God hears the cry of the poor but perhaps bureaucrats don't. In the words of Mother Teresa, we don't wait for government or political leaders, we do it on our own – person to person'.[16]

Certainly, in times of my own personal and professional hardship, the one sure thing that has saved me has been my faith. You get to a point where you don't really care about who God is or what He looks like and whose side He is on. You simply step out into a place that

---

16 Townsend, J. Leadership Beyond Reason (p. 19). Nashville, Tennessee: Thomas Nelson; 2011.

knows almost innately that all will be well, the most terrible tragedy or pain will pass and that somehow healing will follow. It's like nothing else can break you down – there is only one way up and that is by accepting the hand of God's grace that reaches out to anyone who sincerely wants it.

God speaks to us all the time – if we listen. True leadership is about listening, not so much to others, but to God. What is God saying to me, through you? How do I read in between the lines of what you say to me the actual words you use, your tone and manner, your intention and motive, your body language and facial expression? Can I genuinely hear the whisperings of God in my heart, in the silences and pauses, those small spaces in between our words and sentences and each gentle individual breath? Can I recognise and discern what is often left unspoken and feel the way forward knowing that this invisible and powerful force constantly invites and encourages us all to participate in the process? Am I helpful and useful, thinking and acting, devoid of ego, pomp or any form of superiority?

To work on the frontline and to see positive stories of families, young people and kids getting stronger or being reunited with their mob, having access to more opportunities, other people achieving against incredible odds – all of this restores my faith in life and in humanity. This is where God transforms frustration, exasperation and desolation into something very beautiful and powerful.

As Catholics, we open the door for Christ's loving and divine presence when we open our hearts. I am a soul on a sacred journey as are you. Whether we accept or understand this or not is essentially academic. But of course, once we begin to see ourselves as part of this vast cosmos through which God works, our awareness and sense of obligation and responsibility shifts. The love and gratitude for who we are and where we come from is more than just our cultural identity. Differences, antagonism, personalities and short-term political agendas become largely irrelevant. Instead, our inspiration, motivation and solace comes from actively playing our part in this life that God has assigned. We know that we are in the world to make a difference and that is what matters most.

2

FAITH AND WELLBEING
the Hope of Spirituality for Trauma

Fr Frank Brennan SJ AO

Those of us who work in human services often encounter people who are suffering trauma. We need to have an eye to their well-being and our own. Those who work closely with people suffering great trauma run the risk of vicarious trauma. Those who administer human services have a responsibility to care for their staff who are at the forefront assisting trauma sufferers. The trauma may result from unendurable pain or seemingly unforgivable things done to the victim. How to endure the unendurable? How to forgive the unforgivable? Could religion help? Or is it an opiate for the masses which simply disguises the reality that needs to be addressed?

As will be noted in the next contribution there is a lot of literature about well-being. It is accessible to all readers, but particularly suited to those who are atheist or agnostic. Those of us who are religious or spiritual might wonder if we have anything distinctive to add to this discourse. I think we do. We should not be afraid to offer spiritual direction and spiritual conversation to those who seek it.[1] And thus this short paper.

Just prior to the commencement of the 2019 Australian Open

---

1 See https://spiritualdirection.com/2012/11/24/does-emotional-suffering-hinder-spiritual-growth.

Tennis Tournament, the British player Andy Murray gave a teary press conference. He was coming out of surgery. His hip was continuing to cause him grief. He said, 'The pain is too much really. I need to have an end point because I'm playing with no idea of when the pain will stop. I'd like to play until Wimbledon – that's where I'd like to stop playing - but I'm not certain I'm able to do that.'

Those who are suffering trauma are usually weighed down by pain, physical or emotional. At times, it is just too much. They wonder if it can ever end. They are seeking an end point. They would like to achieve some objective, but they doubt that it is ever achievable.

In his book The Psychology of Religion and Coping, Kenneth Parmagent writes:

> 'Only by looking beyond oneself, it is said, can the individual reach out to find intimacy, purpose, and some sense of comfort in living. Only with the help of the sacred can the incomprehensible be understood, the unmanageable managed, and the unbearable endured.'[2]

I have no idea whether Andy Murray is any sort of religious person. But I daresay that if he had a sense of the sacred, then the incomprehensible might seem more understandable, the unmanageable more manageable, and the unbearable more bearable.

All human beings have to face ultimately their mortality, their limitations, their suffering and their existential angst. These things can be daunting and frightening. But they can be faced against a horizon of ultimate meaning and eternal connectedness.

My mother, now no longer with us, lived to her 90s and suffered dementia. She was in care in Sydney. Once I took her in her wheelchair for a walk in the nearby park by the harbour. It was a glorious day. The

---

2 Pargament, K. The psychology of religion and coping. New York: Guilford; 2001. pp. 275-6.

jacarandas were in full bloom. The water was glistening. We stopped at the café for a coffee. I asked Mum, 'How's the coffee?' She didn't have many words those days. She answered, 'Mediocre'. Then her face lit up, and she lifted her arms and looked around and said, 'But this!' She obviously felt blessed to be out in the sunshine, by the water, and with one of her own. Even in a time of ageing and diminishment, life can be a celebration of that horizon, of that perspective. There is so much about our lives which is just so ordinary and mediocre, but we can be buoyed up by that horizon of inclusive love, enduring hope, and sustaining faith.

It's in maintaining that horizon that the spiritual and religious dimension of life might help. The religions of the book – Christianity, Islam and Judaism – are still the most prominent in contemporary Australia. The English lawyer Christopher McCrudden highlights five dimensions that these religions have in common. First, each religion specifies a set of beliefs which are of transcendent importance to believers. Second, each religion promotes a set of values. Third, these values are manifested by practice, both public and private. Fourth, each religion has some institutional structure which authorises particular individuals to maintain orthodoxy and orthopraxis – right thinking and right action. Fifth, each of these religions provides the followers with a social status or social identity. Beliefs, values, practice, institutional structure and social identity can all help an individual maintain a sense of connectedness and wholeness amidst the mess and complexity of daily life.[3]

Fraser Watts, an Anglican priest, psychologist and academic at Cambridge University wrote a book in 2011 entitled Spiritual Healing. His working assumption is that 'if spiritual healing is to be understood, it is important not to neglect the perspectives of either science or

---

3 McCrudden, C. Litigating Religions: An Essay on Human Rights, Courts, and Beliefs. Oxford University Press; 2018. pp. 6, 7.

religion'[4] and this requires 'a framework that is holistic rather than dualistic', seeing 'the spiritual as one facet of an integrated human nature'.[5] No doubt there are many people who are not spiritual or religious who find other ways of living whole, integrated and happy lives even in the midst of trauma. Watts highlights three positive aspects to spirituality:

1. 'Spirituality tends to give people a cognitive framework that enables them to make sense of a broad range of experiences, and to find meaning and significance in them, which seems likely to contribute to healing.'

2. Spirituality is likely 'to be associated with a sense of social support that is conducive to spiritual healing'.

3. By increasing empathy, spirituality 'will in turn lead to an enhanced sense of being upported by others'.[6]

The American psychiatrist Harold Koenig published Faith and Mental Health: Religious Resources of Healing in 2005. Koenig's unashamed starting point is that positive emotions which lift the spirits above the humdrum of ordinary existence are what make life worth living.[7] He highlights the positives and negatives of a religious world view. On the positive side of the ledger, a religious world view can contribute to a sense of hope and optimism: 'Rather than seeing human life as little different from other animals, here today and gone tomorrow, many world religions view men and women as special, created with a divine purpose and having a future beyond the grave.'[8] A religious world view can also give a sense of meaning

---

4 Watts, F. Spiritual Healing. Cambridge University Press; 2011. p. xiii
5 Ibid, 167
6 Ibid, 172
7 Koenig, H. Faith and Mental Health: Religious Resources for Healing. Templeton Press; 2005. p. 50.
8 Ibid, 54

and purpose to life. For example, one recent study of 296 university undergraduates found 'a significant inverse correlation between spiritual factors and boredom-proneness'.[9] A religious world view can also contribute to a greater quality of life especially for people experiencing disability and pain from chronic illness.[10] Koenig quotes various scientific studies which demonstrate that a religious world view can contribute to a range of other positive emotional states including gratefulness, forgiveness, altruism, and social support. But then again there are other studies which indicate some correlation between religion and poor mental health. Those with a strong and perhaps too fundamentalist religious faith might be more prone in some circumstances to exhibit hatred and aggression, prejudice and discrimination, domination over others, dogmatic or obsessive thinking, perfectionism, and undue dependency.

In the Catholic tradition, moral theologians who consider what is necessary for living a good life have turned their attention back to the virtues in recent years. They are focusing less on the objective moral right or wrong of an act and more on the virtues or vices of the actor. The actor does not develop the virtues in a vacuum. Practices, community and narrative all play their role[11]. There is nothing like a good story of an heroic figure to inspire listeners to live a more virtuous life – think only of Martin Luther King or Mother Teresa. Living amongst other virtuous people can help the questing individual to live a better life. It's not a matter of being virtuous on the one big occasion which is a test, but of practising the virtues in season and out of season.

There has long been a debate in neuroscience over 'whether emotions are integrated into conscious, goal oriented thought and

---

9 Ibid, 58

10 Ibid, 60

11 Vogt C. Virtue: Personal Formation and Social Transformation. Theological Studies. 2016;77(1):181-196 188.

activities'¹². Some studies have shown that when a person suffers brain damage only to areas strongly related to emotion and not to areas related to non-affective neural areas, there can still be 'significant impairments in social judgment, practical reasoning, and inter-personal relationships'.¹³ One study concluded that 'rather than dichotomous, opposing systems, what is emerging is a complex interconnection of circuits in which emotional signals cannot be separated from adaptive reasoning and decision making when such judgment and action are relevant for oneself and others'.¹⁴

In his book Human Rights and the Image of God, Roger Ruston offers the useful insight that when religious people speak about human beings created in 'the image of God', this puts 'the human person into a set of relationships: first with God, a relationship of filial adoption and answerability; second, with one another, relationships of equality and respect; third, with the non-human creation, which may be understood as a relationship of stewardship and freedom of use.'¹⁵ This set of relationships can provide a secure horizon against which to negotiate present trauma.

In the mess and complexity of our world, a religious person often finds themselves saying, 'There's nothing more I can do but pray.' The secularist might think they could do more. They might be able. But then again, they might be mistaken. They might then think that prayer could achieve nothing. They may well be right. But at least through prayer, the religious person in that moment of powerlessness is thrown back into that comprehensive world of relationships – with Creator, with humanity, and with the whole of creation. In the words of Australian Governor General, David Hurley, at the 2019 National

---

12 Ibid, 186
13 Ibid, 187
14 Ibid, 187, referring to the study by Michael L Spezio, 'The Neuroscience of emotion and reasoning in social contexts', Modern Theology 27 (2011) 339-356.
15 Ruston R. Human rights and the image of God. London: SCM Press; 2004.p 279

Prayer Breakfast: 'when we pray in times of difficulty, it does not change God, it changes us'.

The web of relationships which is sustaining might just provide the underpinning for healing of the subject who is then empowered to go forth and take on the world making it a better place. The much-published New York rabbi Harold Kushner says, 'A world without God would be a flat, monochromatic world, a world without colour or texture, a world in which all days would be the same. Marriage would be a matter of biology, not fidelity. Old age would be seen as a time of weakness, not of wisdom. In a world like that, we would cast about desperately for any sort of diversion, for any distraction from the emptiness of our lives, because we would never have learned the magic of making some days and some hours special.'[16]

Recently I was performing the baptism of a little baby. Such religious ceremonies nowadays can be a little fraught. The shared narrative of religious belief is not to be presumed. No one, including the priest, quite knows what they are celebrating. At the beginning of the ceremony, the priest traces a small cross on the forehead of the baby, and then invites the parents and godparents to do the same. On this occasion, I realised that all four grandparents were in attendance and so invited them to do the same. I then realised that the baby had two surviving great grandparents who were sitting in the front row of the church. Each was suffering advancing dementia. I invited the parents to present their child to the great grandparents for the tracing of the cross. Everyone knew what to do. Everyone was overjoyed. It was one of those magic moments of which Kushner speaks. Or perhaps what we Catholics would call a sacramental moment – as when I poured the water on the infant's head proclaiming, 'I baptise you in the name of the Father, and of the Son and of the Holy Spirit.' There was a sense in the church that generation to generation to

---

16 Kushner H. Who needs God. New York: Summit Books; 1989.p. 209

generation to generation, a horizon of meaning and love was being lit up for the years ahead, and in the light of all that had gone before.

No doubt physical and psychological pain can be the cause and the symptom of deep trauma. So too the incapacity to forgive. And some things are literally unforgivable. The philosopher Jacques Derrida puts a clear challenge to us:

> Forgiving is surely not to call it quits, clear and discharged. Not oneself, not the other. This would be repeating evil, countersigning it, consecrating it, letting it be what it is, unalterable and identical to itself.

Derrida says:

> it is necessary, it seems to me, to begin from the fact that, yes, there is the unforgivable. Is this not, in truth, the only thing to forgive? The only thing that calls for forgiveness? ... Forgiveness forgives only the unforgivable. One cannot, or should not, forgive; there is only forgiveness, if there is any, where there is the unforgivable. That is to say that forgiveness must announce itself as impossibility itself.[17]

Derrida asserts, 'The forgiveness of the forgivable does not forgive anything: it is not forgiveness.'[18]

Those of us who are Christian accept that there can be no reconciliation between us and God, and therefore no ultimate reconciliation in the ground of our being, except in and through Christ who forgives the unforgiveable. 'It is all God's work; he reconciled us to himself through Christ and gave us the ministry of reconciliation. I mean, God was in Christ reconciling the world to

---

17 Derrida, J. 'On Forgiveness' in On Cosmopolitanism and Forgiveness, New York: Routledge; 2001, pp. 32-33

18 Derrida, J. in 'Hospitality' quoted by Kim L Worthington, 'Suturing the Wound: Derrida's "On Forgiveness" and Schlink's "The Reader"', in Comparative Literature, 2011; 63(2) pp. 203-224 at p. 220

himself, not holding anyone's faults against them, but entrusting to us the message of reconciliation.' (2 Cor 5:18-19)

The reconciliation of this vertical relationship is possible only through the mediation of Jesus who embodies, lives and dies the reality of this reconciliation. He puts us right with our God and thereby establishes the basis for right relationships with each other. Those of the most profoundly humanitarian and humanist bent might profess profound commitment to truth and justice. But if forgiveness be the possibility of forgiving the unforgivable, this cannot be reckoned or achieved in the secular public forum.

This troubling question arises in Ian McEwan's popular novel *Atonement*. The main character Briony as a child wrongly accuses her older sister's boyfriend of a dreadful wrongdoing while he is visiting the family estate in the English countryside. Years later after he has wrongly served a term in prison, he then goes to war, escapes from Dunkirk and meets up again with Briony and the older sister. In the novel, Briony is an accomplished novelist and the last chapter consists of her ruminations about how to recount the tale and how to have it end. After publication of the book, McEwan confided that early in the writing project, he had read the initial chapters to his wife who then asked how it was all going to end. He started to improvise: 'I told her the last chapter and to my amazement she burst into tears. Ah, well, I thought, this is correct. I hadn't seen it in quite so emotional terms.'[19] It was another two years before he wrote his final chapter and in terms almost identical to what he had described to his wife. In this closing chapter, Briony, the all controlling novelist within the novel, writes what McEwan had in mind those last two years:

> The problem these fifty-nine years has been this: how can a novelist achieve atonement when, with her absolute power

---

19 'Atoning for his past' *The Age*, 5 May 2002, at https://www.theage.com.au/entertainment/books/atoning-for-his-past-20020505-gdu6hx.html

of deciding outcomes, she is also God? There is no one, no entity or higher form that she can appeal to, or be reconciled with, or that can forgive her. There is nothing outside her. In her imagination, she has set the limits and the terms. No atonement for God, or novelists, even if they are atheists. It was always an impossible task, and that was precisely the point. The attempt was all.[20]

Originally McEwan had named his novel An Atonement. However, on reading it, Oxford Professor Timothy Garton Ash 'suggested that he remove the 'an', because the novel was not just about Briony's search for atonement but a more generic sense of redemption, about guilt as something "too great to expiate".'[21]

The religious person who is Christian is able to commit to a mission for reconciliation. They affirm their belief that in Christ the unforgivable is forgiven and that even the guilt which can be too great to expiate can be the occasion for redemption. This is when together we know what we are, and can go on (immersed in the marketplace of politics, political correctness, conflict and avoidance), finding in ourselves and the other, the sacred meeting place of justice, truth, mercy and peace.

To do this we need moments and places that bridge the gap of difference by placing borders anonymously around the gaps of difference without spelling out the points of difference within those borders. Neither the victor nor the victim can set the limits and the terms. Together and equally at risk, we might embrace the possibility of being and encountering the reconciler, the reconciled and the member of the reconciling community.

Those of us who find fruit in the spiritual or religious when

---

20 McEwan, I. Atonement, Jonathan Cape, 2001, 371.
21 'Atoning for his past' The Age, 5 May 2002, at https://www.theage.com.au/entertainment/books/atoning-for-his-past-20020505-gdu6hx.html

confronting trauma always need to have the humility to accept that others without religion or spirituality may find a way to forgive the unforgivable or to endure the unendurable. But those who see life as relational and graced are privileged to have at their disposal additional spiritual practices, community and narrative. This allows the traumatised subject to endure unbearable pain, find joy in the mediocre and embrace new possibilities, which include embracing the realities of diminishment, suffering and even death.

3

FINDING THE LANGUAGE
Theory and Terms from the Secular Literature

Brenton Prosser PhD

I have a favourite activity that I like to use when facilitating workshops. I ask everyone in the room to stand up, then instruct them to sit down when the statement that I make is no longer true.

"I have been working in the sector for one year... for two years... for five years... etc". Once I get to twenty years, there are usually some laughs around the room. Invariably, when working with the social services sectors, a large group is still standing at thirty years. But I usually stop before forty years - some people might give away that they look younger than they are!

The questions that I rarely get to ask of such leaders is: "How do you do it?" "How have you sustained your service?"

When I do, people are often self-effacing. They say that "they are no-one special". "It's tough, but they just plug away". Some explain they come from a family with strong commitment to service, that they were inspired by a particular person at a key time in their life, or that they are motivated by religious belief.

But if I push further to ask, "No, really, how do you do it?" people find it difficult. They often struggle to find the words. This may be due to my questions that probe parts of oneself that we do not usually talk about. In fact, many of us were trained in a model of rational professionalism that actively discouraged such personal conversations. However, in this contribution, my aim is to suggest some new language to prompt such conversations.

In this essay I want to discuss the irony in the profession, that is, where significant importance is given to human service workers caring for their clients, but often much less is given to caring for the carer.[1] For some time, I've explored academic work around how to help social service professionals to thrive working in contexts of conflict, poverty, trauma and tragedy.[2] In the following pages, I share some of these insights.

Everyday conversations

Some of the words we use to talk about our professional work have been around for some time. Take resilience, wellness and wellbeing as examples.

Resilience

In classical mythology, the symbol of resilience was a reed in the river because of its capacity to sway in the breeze and withstand fierce wind storms. The origins of the modern word come from the Latin 'resilire' which means to rebound or return to the original form. Today, it is usually associated with the capacity to 'bounce back' or 'bounce back better' and is used everywhere from individual psychology to

---

[1] Wendt S, Tuckey M, Prosser B. Thriving, not just surviving, in emotionally demanding fields of practice. Health & Social Care in the Community. 2011;19(3):317-325.

[2] Prosser B. Knowledge of the Heart: Ethical Implications of Sociological Research With Emotion. Emotion Review. 2014;7(2):175-180.; Prosser B, Tuckey M, Wendt S. Affect and the lifeworld: Conceptualising surviving and thriving in the human service professions. Health Sociology Review. 2013;22(3):318-327.; Prosser B. Critical pedagogy and the mythopoetic: a case study from Adelaide's northern urban fringe. In: Leonard T, Willis P, ed. by. Pedagogies of the Imagination: mythopoetic curriculum in educational practice. Dordrecht: Springer Press; 2020. p. 208-222.

community capacity, economic crises to emergency management.

The close association of the term with the social service professions started in the 1970's. Psychologists[3] first used the term as a way to identify the protective factors for psychological health. It wasn't long before it was redefined as the ability to function in immensely demanding settings and linked with the notion of stress.[4]

As awareness grew around the personally and professionally demanding nature of service work, the question facing those supporting social service professionals was how to "increase" their resilience. The answer they came up with was to develop stronger professional identity through pre-service and in-service training. The idea was the stronger your professional identity, the more resilient you will be.

Wellness and wellbeing

Wellness is used extensively within social service policy and programs, and increasingly embraced by the corporate world through mindfulness initiatives for employees. However, because its use is so broad, it also makes it difficult to define.

An early definition of 'wellness' emerged in the 1950's via the idea of active health through lifestyle change. Wellness tends to be used to describe a state of overall physical health, while wellbeing includes mental health in its definition. The path to wellbeing is to be found through holistic models, which encompasses the physiological, mental, emotional, social, spiritual, and occupational state of individuals.[5]

---

3 Werner E, Bierman J, French F. The children of Kauai. Honolulu: University of Hawaii Press; 1971.

4 Norris F, Tracy M, Galea S. Looking for resilience: Understanding the longitudinal trajectories of responses to stress. Social Science & Medicine. 2009;68(12):2190-2198.

5 See: https://en.wikipedia.org/wiki/Well-being

An important influence on the recent expansion of these ideas was the emergence of positive psychology in the 1990's. This body of work was a deliberate response to the focus on mental illness, negative thinking and deficit labels within mainstream psychology.[6] It represented a growing recognition of the importance of positive and adaptive psychological states (e.g., happiness and resilience) in promoting health and wellbeing.[7] It also identified the predictors of wellbeing as high self-esteem, and claimed more could be learned from success rather than failure.

There are some common criticisms of these ideas. One is that happiness, wellbeing and wellness are self-reported and can be hard to measure objectively. For instance, as a person's awareness of wellbeing grows so may their expectations. Alternatively, if they are under significant stress their perceptions may be negatively tainted. Both of which means that they may report lower wellbeing assessments even though there has been improvement. Another, is that wellness and wellbeing models can use measurement tools that do not capture diversity and assumes one size fits all.[8] Perhaps the most important for the discussion in this book, is that unless the term spirituality is overtly stated, wellbeing is usually a solely secular term.

Stress and burnout

Back in the 1930's, clinical researcher Hans Selye was the first to define stress in a form that we would recognise today. He defined stress as the body's response to changing demands. His laboratory work showed that exposing subjects to the same demanding stimuli

---

6   See: https://positivepsychologyprogram.com/founding-fathers/
7   Seligman M, Csikszentmihalyi M. Positive psychology: An introduction. American Psychologist. 2000;55(1):5-14.
8   Held B. The Negative Side of Positive Psychology. Journal of Humanistic Psychology. 2004;44(1):9-46.

produced the same physiological responses, while doing so repeatedly results in sickness or disease. Today, stress has evolved in popular terms to represent the physical, mental or emotional strain humans experience due to a perception that demands on them are greater than their individual capacity to meet them.

Despite its popular currency, stress is not a particularly useful term across social service professions. First, the term is broad and second, it is subjective and has no external reference point for measurement. Third, it is inherently negative and focusses only on the size of the challenge and the vulnerability of the individual. Fourth, it is now embedded in a public discourse where stress is a prominent feature of modern life.[9] While an individual may find it useful to say they are stressed, it does little to lead to recovery and the label itself can be a barrier to exiting that state.

Researchers have tried to address some of these limitations. One concept that emerged in the 1970's was 'burnout'.[10] In short, burnout was the result of long-term unresolvable job stress. This research moved from describing a subjective state and physical response to measuring levels of exhaustion and illness from excessive work demands. More recently in the health and human service professions, 'compassion fatigue' has been described as a form of burnout resulting from the personal cost from caring for clients who expose professionals regularly to negative emotion, trauma and tragedy.[11] 'Burnout' is now commonplace amongst the professional lexicon and has increasingly been taken up by research in the professional

---

9 Prosser B, Tuckey M, Wendt S. The personal domain: Exploring what sustains professionals in urban fringe communities. Canberra: Australian Association for Research in Education Conference; 2009.

10 Freudenberger H. Staff burnout. Journal of Social Issues. 1974;30(1).

11 Adams R, Boscarino J, Figley C. Compassion fatigue and psychological distress among social workers: A validation study. American Journal of Orthopsychiatry. 2006;76(1):103-108.

disciplines.[12] This is largely because it is a more useful reworking of the stress concept.

Another approach has been to specify the sub-set of 'work stress.' This was the focus of work within the occupational health sciences and organisational psychology between the 1960s and 1990s.[13] Emerging out of reformist movements that emphasised democratic and socially responsible work arrangements, this work sought better lives (and less stress) for workers. Increasingly, researchers looked at everyday factors affecting work stress, including occupational stress models and/or risk factors. This led to a growing emphasis on the role of organisations in expanding or mitigating these factors. The benefit of this perspective is that it provides scope to shift beyond the individual and highlights the need for organisational response to support improved individual outcomes. The drawback, however, is that this literature still largely sees situations in terms of negative experiences, individual threats, organisational hindrances or significant challenges.[14]

Unfortunately, all of the above terms, while popular, are not particularly helpful in opening up new perspectives with human service professionals. This is because they do little to empower leaders

---

12 Schwartz R., Tiamiyu M. & Dwyer D. Social worker hope and perceived burnout: the effects of age, years in practice, and setting. Administration in Social Work. 2007; 31 (4), 103–119; Coyle D., Edwards D., Hannigan B., Fothergill A. & Burnard P. A systematic literature review of stress among mental health social workers. International Social Work. 2005; 48 (2), 201–211; Van den Broeck A., Vansteenkiste M., De Witte H. & Lens W. Explaining the relationships between job characteristics, burnout, and engagement: the role of basic psychological need satisfaction. Work and Stress. 2008; 22 (3), 277–294.

13 Väänänen, A., J. Turtiainen, E. Anttila, and P. Varje. Formulation of work stress in 1960–2000: analysis of scientific works from the perspective of historical sociology. Social Science Medicine. 2012; 75(5): 784–794.

14 Tuckey, M. R., Searle, B., Boyd, C. M., Winefield, A. H., & Winefield, H. R. Hindrances are not threats: Advancing the multidimensionality of work stress. Journal of Occupational Health Psychology. 2015; 20(2), 131.

and workers to think, reflect, plan and transform.[15]

Professional discussions

Beyond the popular discourses, there are also a range of terms and concepts that are used regularly within the service professions and associated academic disciplines. Let's start with one that was mentioned above – professional identity.

Professional identity

To have a 'strong' professional identity is to align your personal identity closely with that of a specific profession. The strength of your professional identity is revealed by how convincingly and consistently you embody it in public and private life. For some it is all encompassing, for others they are able to switch between identities according to context. Where it can be difficult for some is when your professional identity is the only one that others see you through (e.g., the only general practitioner in a county town). Another is negotiating an emphasis on professional objectivity and rationality in times of high emotional demand, especially when working in professions that include care and empathy as part of best practice.[16] One potential product of such situations has been identified as 'emotional dissonance'. This term was first coined by Janz and Timmers[17] as the

---

15 Harkness, A., Long, B., Bermbach, N., Patterson, K., Jordan, S., & Kahn, H. Talking about work stress: Discourse analysis and implications for stress interventions. Work & Stress. 2005; 19(2), 121–136.

16 Zembylas, M. Caring for teacher emotion: Reflections on teacher self-development. Studies in philosophy and education. 2003; 22(2), 103-125; Yin, H. B., & Lee, J. C. K. Emotions matter: Teachers' feelings about their interactions with teacher trainers during curriculum reform. Chinese Education & Society. 2011; 44(4), 82-97.

17 Jansz J, Timmers M. Emotional Dissonance. Theory & Psychology. 2002;12(1):79-95.

feeling of unease that comes when one supresses an emotion because it does not align with what professional identity allows. This has been associated over the longer term with burnout.[18]

I believe the professional identity concept is not particularly useful beyond its initial insight. In reality, most people's lives are too complex and their identities multiple and too fluid to expect them to align consistently with one distinct identity. We are constantly inhabiting many, sometimes blurred, identities that change and blend according to the context and the audience; seeking to deeply embed people into one ideal professional identity type is at best unrealistic and at its worst harmful.

Emotional labour

Those who are familiar with scholarship within the human and social service disciplines will be aware of the term 'emotional labour'. This emerged from the work of Arlie Hochschild in the 1980s. Emotional labour represented a breakthrough in thinking and led to a new wave of scientific interest around the role of emotion in the service professions. Hochschild[19] defined emotional labour as the commercialisation of emotions through expectations that workers produce them to meet organisation standards or elicit customer response. She explained that in the service professions this was not a choice of the employee but a key expectation of their employment. In these professions, employers purchased not only your skills but also your emotional state.

The way Hochschild saw this working was through the operation of emotional cultures which set the rules around what employees are

---

18 Hopp, H., Rohrmann, S., Zapf, D., & Hodapp, V. Psychophysiological effects of emotional dissonance in a face-to-face service interaction. Anxiety, Stress, & Coping. 2010;23(4), 399-414.

19 Hochschild A. The Managed Heart. Berkeley: University of California Press; 2012.

expected to feel. Of course, people do not always feel the way that the workplace rules dictate. It is difficult to feel equally positive toward every client and as happy at the end of the day as you were at the start. So people perform superficial efforts to mask one's true feelings; this is described as surface acting, while efforts to suppress or alter feelings over time is deep acting.[20] In Hochschild's view, this emotional acting, performed as part of one's paid work, was seen to be harmful over time.[21] While these ideas initially applied only to retail services, they soon came to be applied to human service professions.[22]

There is large body of research around emotional labour – too large to review here. But it has been seen as a useful concept. Some of the benefits have been that it gives more detailed insight into how emotional demands operate in work contexts. It has highlighted the commercial role of what some have called "softer skills". It has also been used to draw more attention to how the emotion and empathy of professionals often drive action that covers up or compensates for system, funding or organisational limitations, particularly in the health and human services.[23]

Emotional intelligence and regulation

Amongst the revisionists are those who have explored forms of emotional management. This work looks at how professionals modify emotions by re-evaluating a situation before emotions are generated

---

20 Hochschild, A. R. Ideology and emotion management: A perspective and path for future research. Research agendas in the sociology of emotions. 1990: 117, 117-142.
21 Ibid.
22 For example: Staden, H. Alertness to the needs of others: a study of the emotional labour of caring. Journal of advanced nursing, 1998; 27(1), 147-156; Lavee, E., & Strier, R. Social workers' emotional labour with families in poverty: Neoliberal fatigue? Child & Family Social Work, 2018; 23(3), 504-512.
23 Bolton, S. C. Getting to the heart of the emotional labour process: a reply to Brook. Work, employment and society, 2009; 23(3), 549-560.

(emotional regulation). It also considers a professional's capacity to generate emotions, and use this ability to foster one's own and others' emotional and intellectual development (emotional intelligence).

What these 'emotional labour' insights offer us in our work supporting staff and colleagues is a different way of looking at the interplay between organisation and individual. While not drawing attention away from the importance of adaptive emotional regulation or developing emotional intelligence, it calls on us to examine the structures, processes and cultures that demand acting or constrain individuals.[24] It provides us with a starting point for better analysis to align efforts for emotional support across all levels of our organisations.

Some less familiar ideas

Let's now turn to some lesser known terms, such as lifeworld, affect and the mythopoetic.

Lifeworld

The term 'lifeworld' has emerged from the critique of the popular term 'work-life balance'. Lifeworld places its two components in competitive tension implying work is paid (and negative) and life is unpaid (and positive), while mobile technology increasingly blurs our work and out of work lives.[25] Work-life balance can undervalue the

---

24 Perrewé P, Rosen C, Halbesleben J. The role of emotion and emotion regulation in job stress and well being. Bingley, UK: Emerald; 2013.
25 Prosser, B., Tuckey, M. & Wendt, S. 'Affect and the lifeworld: conceptualising surviving and thriving in the human service professions', Health Sociology Review. 2013; 22(3), 318-327

commercial value of life work,[26] whether that be through domestic responsibilities or drawing on the personal domain to sustain one's work.[27] Work-life balance places the emphasis on the individual to do the balancing,[28] and not enough on consideration of system factors.[29] By contrast, 'lifeworld' hones in on the integration of all aspects of life, including work.

'Lifeworld' explores how experiences, ideologies, beliefs, values and other life resources work in ways that help people to flourish as professionals.[30] It's important not to confuse the term with others like the everyday or private life. The lifeworld is experienced before we think about it, it is subjective (often emotional) and usually taken for granted.[31]

The term lifeworld can be useful as it opens up a set of unacknowledged but motivating and sustaining resources that people draw on in their work. It has the potential to open up new perspectives on what personal elements of life empowers work, provides connections and sustains vocation. It can also support new ways of

---

26 Pocock B, Skinner N, Williams P. Work–life outcomes in Australia: Concepts, outcomes and policy. In: Warhurst C, Eikhof D, Haunschild A, ed. by. Work less, live more? Critical analysis of the work–life boundary. New York: Palgrave MacMillan; 2008. p. 22-43. Pocock, B. Work-life 'balance' in Australia: Limited progress, dim prospects. Asia Pacific Journal of Human Resources, 2005; 43(2), 198-209.

27 Wendt, S., Tuckey, M. & Prosser, B. 'Thriving, not just surviving, in emotionally demanding fields of practice', Health & Social Care in the Community, 2011;19(3), 317-325.

28 Williams, P., Pocock, B., & Skinner, N. Clawing back time: Expansive working time and implications for work–life outcomes in Australian workers. Work, Employment and Society, 2009; 22(4), 737–748

29 Rigby, M., & O'Brien-Smith, F. Trade union interventions in work-life balance. Work, Employment and Society, 2010; 24(2), 203–220.

30 Wendt, S., Tuckey, M. & Prosser, B. 'Thriving, not just surviving, in emotionally demanding fields of practice', Health & Social Care in the Community, 2011; 19(3), 317-325.

31 Husserl, E. The crisis of European sciences. Evanston, IL: Northwest University Press; 1970.

thinking about how we sustain our work through difficult times. I would argue that its greatest limitation is that it can be elusive or hard to describe. In practical terms, it can also be a useful resource when assessing human service professional practice through approaches such as participatory action research.

Affect

Another, even more abstract, concept is that of 'affect'. Often confused with effect, emotion or powerful feelings, it is actually quite different.

At its simplest, affect is about the unconscious and motivating connections between people. It is defined as our unconscious and immersive responses to beauty, tragedy, love and trauma.[32] Affect is seen as a collective force that emphasises human dignity and connection and is expressed through emotion, empathy and positive engagement with our world.

I think 'affect' can be considered in two different ways. One is similar to what Sebastian Smee describes as a sustaining inner life within a whirling world of technology.

> The inner life is obscurely affected by the weather and atmospheric pressure. Perhaps also by an early traumatic experience, the last great book you read, your most recent humiliation or the last intensely beautiful person you saw in the street, but all this in a way you would struggle to ever put into words.[33]

It comes into play when we feel ourselves strongly connected with

---

32 Massumi, B. Parables for the virtual: Movement, affect, sensation. London, England: Duke University Press; 2002.

33 Smee, S. Quarterly Essay 72 Net Loss: The Inner Life in the Digital Age 2018: 72. Black Inc.

things, people or works of art that are outside of us but have power inside of us. It is a much more complex, mysterious, deeper and sustaining of self than past scholars often give us credit for.

The other aspect of affect is that it relates to deep human connections. It is why natural disasters bring out acts of bravery and generosity from strangers. It is why the experience of being a parent can change your emotional responses to what you see in movies. It is why we come to connect with people that are very different to us.

This concept can be elusive and hard to discuss, but it speaks to something that many of those in the human services understand, that there are deep connections between humans that can drive and sustain their work. This term too can be a source to open up professional reflection, research and learning.

Mythopoetic

Another term, which may at first appear obscure, has potential for exploring what helps professionals thrive in their work; this is 'mythopoetic'. The value in this term is that it is perhaps the closest secular term for what others might call spirituality. The easiest way to understand it is to break it into its component parts.

'Mythos' refers to narrative, particularly large stories that explain social phenomena, while 'poesis' refers to creativity, particularly through the spoken word and emotion. Looked at in this way, Christian faith provides one of the best examples of a meta-narrative that explains human activity and passion in service. One of the underpinnings of this concept is to reverse one of the most influential ideas of the Renaissance by reunifying body, mind and spirit back into one. Some have described this as rediscovering the knowledge of the heart,[34] which can be seen as motivating the head, heart and hand to support social change.[35]

For example, in times of struggle, one can look to the example of Christ, who in taking on the sins of the world understands the depths of hardship and trauma beyond that of which any one of us can experience. One can look to God's eternal plan of which vocation and service (and the heartache that comes with it) is a part. Also, as we look to Scripture, one can see the healing hand of God throughout history, which can give confidence that when our service comes at a physical cost, there is always hope for healing.

In practice, mythopoetic is a concept that can open up reflection on our respective calling to service and good works, our sense of vocation, and our deeply held passion for social justice. The practical challenge it presents, however is its abstract conception. However, its exploration can lead to insight and reflection on what inspires and sustains us through tough times.

Conclusion

At the end of this brief review of the terms we find in the secular literature I am hoping that the reader will have a stronger understanding of the complex concepts woven throughout the contributions within this book. I also hope that it will enable us to find familiarity with these popular and secular concepts and that they can lead to conversations with leaders and with staff around the sustenance of our social service workforce.

---

34 Hillman, J. The Thought of the Heart. Texas: Spring Publications; 1981. Leonard, T., & Willis, P. (Eds.). Pedagogies of the imagination: Mythopoetic curriculum in educational practice. Springer Science & Business Media; 2008.

35 Prosser, B. Chapter 15: Critical pedagogy and the mythopoetic: a case study from Adelaide's northern urban fringe, in T. Leonard & P. Willis (eds.), Pedagogies of the Imagination: mythopoetic curriculum in educational practice, Dordrecht: Springer Press, 2008. pp.203-222.

There is a growing synergy between the spiritual and secular in scholarship concerning social service and the sustaining of a committed and effective workforce. Recognition of this synergy within organisations and across our sector has the potential to be the catalyst to explore how spirituality can empower and sustain us both individually and collectively.

4

CARING AT THE COALFACE
Researching Empathetic Labour and Vicarious Resilience[1]

Jonathon Louth PhD

It's a side effect of empathy I think; we're all going to get it at some level. It's a spectrum I think, vicarious trauma, we're all going to get affected by other people's stuff just based on being empathetic human beings.

Frontline worker (focus group participant)

We walk alongside the clients. We listen to those stories. We invest emotionally. We are human, so it has to have an impact.

---

1 This chapter is based on the longer TAASE research report: 'Understanding vicarious trauma: Exploring cumulative stress, fatigue and trauma in a frontline community services setting,' available at http://centacare.org.au/wp-content/uploads/corporate/VicariousTraumaReport.pdf. Jonathon acknowledges the co-authors of that report: Tanya Mackay for her assistance with developing the initial literature review; George Karpetis for his SPSS analysis of the ProQOL validated survey results, and Ian Goodwin-Smith for conceptual contributions. Jonathon also extends his gratitude to the Centacare Catholic Family Services (CCFS) project team members Megan Welsh, Jacqueline Amos, Lesley Donnelly, Gayle Tourish, Tracy Ingram and Leeanne Kays. This gratitude is also extended to Elizabeth Rowe and Pauline Connolly.

Frontline worker (focus group participant)

Working with traumatised clients results in very real consequences for human service professionals. With the effects well noted, vicarious trauma, compassion fatigue and burnout are three categories of the psychological consequences of empathetic labour.[2] With the rapid expansion of the community services sector over the past few decades, frontline workers are experiencing higher levels of trauma that will impact their everyday lives well into the future.

Serious consideration needs to be given to the emerging generation of veterans who are returning – not from war – but from working within vulnerable communities and families within our cities, suburbs, regions and remotely. This situation is a 'ticking time bomb' that cannot and should not be ignored by governments, funding bodies and service providers.

Working closely with Centacare Catholic Family Services (CCFS) in Adelaide, researchers from The Australian Alliance for Social Enterprise (TAASE) at the University of South Australia undertook an 18-month organisational-wide study into the cumulative effects of vicarious trauma. While clear areas of improvement were identified, the overall rate of traumatisation among CCFS staff was low. Further, the study also identified the empathetic abilities of staff. Overall, the findings reflected a unique alignment between Centacare's purpose and mission and the capabilities of staff, many workers' very notion of 'self', and their ability to embrace vicarious resilience.

---

2   Adams, R. E., Boscarino, J. A. & Figley, C. R. Compassion Fatigue and Psychological Distress Among Social Workers: A Validation Study. American Journal of Orthopsychiatry. 2006; 76(1), 103-108.

Vicarious trauma, compassion fatigue and burnout.

Emotional labour,[3] which defines much of what is performed by social workers and related helper professions, can come at a cost. While providing services and supports to clients who have experienced trauma can be highly rewarding, the consequences of doing so are also an occupational hazard. 'Vicarious traumatisation' describes the range of cumulative and harmful effects on an individual who has been exposed to, and has empathetically engaged with other people's trauma.[4] Moreover, it can manifest emotionally and physically in a manner that an individual's perception of themselves, others and the world is altered.[5]

'Compassion fatigue' is a reduction in the interest and capacity of human service workers to empathise with the suffering of those they work with.[6] This reflects the exhaustion and emotional impact that can come from empathetic engagement, which can have particularly adverse effects upon workers.[7] As was also shown with this study,

---

3   See Chapter 2.
4   Baird, K., & Kracen, A. C. Vicarious traumatization and secondary traumatic stress: A research synthesis. Counselling Psychology Quarterly, 2006; 19(2), 181-188; McCann, I.L., & Pearlman, L.A. Vicarious traumatization: a framework for understanding the psychological effects of working with victims. Journal of Traumatic Stress, 1990;3(1), 131-149; Pearlman, L., & MacIan, P. Vicarious traumatization: An empirical study on the effects of trauma work on trauma therapists. Professional Psychology: Research and Practice, 1995; 26(6), 558-565.
5   Devilly, G. J., Wright, R., & Varker, T. Vicarious trauma, secondary traumatic stress or simply burnout? Effect of trauma therapy on mental health professionals. Australian and New Zealand Journal of Psychiatry, 2009; 43(4), 373-385; Pearlman, L., & MacIan, P. Vicarious traumatization: An empirical study on the effects of trauma work on trauma therapists. Professional Psychology: Research and Practice, 1995; 26(6), 558-565; Trippany, R. L., White Kress, V. E., & Wilcoxon, S.A. Preventing vicarious trauma: What counselors should know when working with trauma survivors. Journal of Counseling & Development, 2004; 82, 31-37.
6   See Chapter 2.
7   Adams, R. E., Boscarino, J. A. & Figley, C. R. Compassion Fatigue and Psychological Distress Among Social Workers: A Validation Study. American Journal of Orthopsychiatry, 2006; 76(1), 103-108.

there is a very strong correlation between compassion fatigue and work satisfaction. A takeaway from this study is for organisations to consider how appropriate interventions will encourage healthier workplaces that will benefit workers and clients alike.

Like vicarious trauma, compassion fatigue is cumulative, yet it differs in the manner in which it contributes to the wearing down of empathy and compassion. It is an empathetic exhaustion that stems from dealing with distressing and emotional circumstances and material that define the daily work of professional caregivers.[8] Moreover, these reactions share a similarity with post-traumatic stress disorder (PTSD) and have interchangeably been labelled as secondary traumatic stress.

As such, there is a substantive point of difference: vicarious trauma represents an empathetic bonding, while compassion fatigue is more commonly associated with empathetic erosion. However, symptomatically, they are similar in the manifestation of 'feelings of emotional depletion, helplessness and isolation' that mimic the 'direct trauma survivor' (p. 6).[9]

'Burnout' is a concept that is also interwoven with vicarious trauma, secondary traumatic stress and compassion fatigue within the literature.[10] However, burnout can be experienced more broadly and relates to exhaustion or stress from difficult clients or roles rather than exposure to a client's traumatic experience. Burnout results in detachment, depersonalisation and a reduced sense of accomplishment and/or commitment to a job. Like vicarious trauma, burnout can manifest physically, emotionally or behaviourally and

---

8   Newell, J.M., Nelson-Gardell, D., & MacNeil, G. Clinician Responses to Client Traumas: A Chronological Review of Constructs and Terminology. Traumatic Violence Abuse, 2016; 17(3), 306-313.

9   Kadambi, M. A., & Ennis, L. Reconsidering vicarious trauma: A review of the literature and its' limitations. Journal of Trauma Practice, 2004; 3(2), 1-21.

10 See Chapter 2.

impact professional and personal relationships.[11]

The important point of difference is that burnout is transient and preventable. Vicarious trauma, on the other hand, is an unavoidable consequence of working with trauma survivors.[12] Hence, mitigating and ameliorating the effects of vicarious trauma needs to be a core concern of frontline community sector organisations. In doing so, burnout – which can be a consequence of or a compounding factor – will and should be addressed through a developed suite of strategies.

Birds of a feather?

While it is possible to differentiate between these closely related concepts, there is debate about these experiences and their symptomology. For some, vicarious trauma must be acknowledged as a unique experience.[13] Others note the interchangeability of the terms (including secondary traumatic stress) in previous research, yet they maintain that vicarious trauma is a specific phenomenon concerned only with people who experience trauma through exposure to clients' traumatic material.[14]

Irrespective of these debates there is a clear consensus that

---

11 Devilly, G. J., Wright, R., & Varker, T. Vicarious trauma, secondary traumatic stress or simply burnout? Effect of trauma therapy on mental health professionals. Australian and New Zealand Journal of Psychiatry, 2009; 43(4), 373-385; Maslach, C. (1982). Burnout: the cost of caring. Englewood Cliffs, NJ: Prentice Hall; Tabor, P. D. Vicarious traumatization: Concept analysis. Journal of Forensic Nursing, 2011; 7(4), 203-208.

12 Kadambi, M. A., & Ennis, L. Reconsidering vicarious trauma: A review of the literature and its' limitations. Journal of Trauma Practice, 2004; 3(2), 1-21.

13 Tabor, P. D. Vicarious traumatization: Concept analysis. Journal of Forensic Nursing, 2011; 7(4), 203-208.

14 Dunkley, J., & Whelan, T. A. Vicarious traumatisation: Current status and future directions. British Journal of Guidance & Counseling, 2006; 34(1), 107-116.

exposure to traumatic material impacts helping professionals.[15] Moreover, the caring and helping professions are at the frontline of a field that is undergoing a rapid expansion, which is underscored by an increasing need for their services. Workers are experiencing higher rates of secondary exposure to violence, abuse, torture, war/terrorism trauma, sexual violence, childhood abuse, and natural disasters due to the nature and expansion of their work. Cumulative empathetic engagement across this spectrum of issues increases the risk for workers; the consequences of which increases the likelihood of fear, anxiety, sadness, anger or disappointment unhealthily manifesting. Further, there is the very real risk that this may impact how the frontline worker view themselves, others and society.[16]

From this perspective, the study applied a broad lens that allowed for a wide-reaching engagement with CCFS staff across experiences and effects that have stemmed from secondary exposure to traumatic material. Taking this approach accommodated for the individualised and different nature of what staff described as "trauma".

Can strength be found through trauma?

While trauma is transformational, its impact is not exclusively negative. Stories of resilience and positive growth that emerge from some traumatic episodes have been shown to positively alter life narratives, inspire communities and have a positive impact on workers. In this sense, it can actually become a source of strength for workers.

As a concept, vicarious resilience emerged from a study that examined the experiences of psychotherapists who worked with

---

15 Howlett, S. L. & Collins, A. Vicarious traumatisation: risk and resilience among crisis support volunteers in a community organisation. South African Journal of Psychology, 2014; 44(2), 180-190.

16 Sexton, L. Vicarious traumatisation of counsellors and effects on their workplaces. British Journal of Guidance and Counselling, 1999; 27(3).

survivors and the families of survivors of political violence. Stories of adaptation and survival, of reciprocity in the face of adversity emerged as a source of inspiration.[17] These experiences can similarly be linked with post-traumatic growth and compassion satisfaction where meaning and purpose is enhanced through exposure to trauma.[18] In short, this 'resilience effect' reflects the positive affect that clients can have on workers, which, in turn, adds to the value that can be gained from caring work (see Hernandez-Wolfe).[19]

For community sector organisations, the idea of vicarious resilience should be viewed with increasing relevance. This shift in focus will help organisations extend beyond simply identifying preventative measures and avoidance strategies and encourage the development of vicarious resilience strategies. This study, conducted in partnership between TAASE and CCFS, aimed to elevate vicarious resilience as a pillar of a strength-based approach to working with trauma and its impacts.

The results: what we looked at

Utilising the professional quality of life (ProQOL) validated survey[20] we produced an organisational baseline for vicarious traumatisation.

---

17 Hernandez-Wolfe, P., Gangsei, D. & Engstrom, D. Vicarious resilience: A new concept in work with those who survive trauma. Family Process, 2007; 46(2), pp. 229-241.

18 Hyatt-Burkhart, D. The experience of vicarious posttraumatic growth in mental health workers. Journal of Loss and Trauma, 2014; 19(5), pp. 452-461; Frey, L., Beesley, D., Abott, D. & Kendrick, E. Vicarious Resilience in Sexual Assault and Domestic Violence Advocates. Psychological Trauma: Theory, Research, Practice, and Policy, 2017; 9(1), pp. 44-51.

19 Hernandez-Wolfe, P., Gangsei, D. & Engstrom, D. Vicarious resilience: A new concept in work with those who survive trauma. Family Process, 2007; 46(2), pp. 229-241.

20 Stamm, B. H. The concise ProQOL manual (2nd ed.): Pocatello, ID: proqol. org. 2010.

Measuring for burnout out, secondary traumatisation stress and compassion satisfaction, we were able to show that vicarious trauma was not a systemic issue with CCFS.

The baseline allows for both cross sectoral and internal longitudinal comparisons. Importantly, this will allow CCFS to measure and plot vicarious trauma in the future, allowing for the testing of specific policy approaches. While the instrument provides an excellent baseline that can be used to compare both across the sector and longitudinally (should it be deployed internally and consistently over time), it does not provide a deep qualitative inquiry into workers affective experiences. Emotional toil is not always easily captured in a survey.

A series of in-depth focus groups with staff from across the organisation were vital to explain the ProQOL results and to explore and identify the protective factors and the potential stressors that may undermine those factors. The focus groups clearly identified a number of recurring themes that spoke to the traumatic nature of their work, why they do the work, and what they need to feel supported in their work. It is on this that I wish to turn my focus.

Depth and discovery: listening to the staff voice

An in-depth analysis of staff voices within CCFS allowed the researchers to identify five key themes (and a substantial number of sub-themes). They were:

1. Vicarious trauma (absorption)
2. Workload (exhaustion)
3. Support (care)
4. Job satisfaction (meaningfulness)
5. Structural factors (indifference)

Shifting from the breadth of the survey to the depth of qualitative engagements allowed for the correlation of data across themes and revealed the nature and make-up of protective factors, the prevalence of risk and the formal and informal mitigation of that risk. Finally – and perhaps most importantly – the focus groups reflected the need for the recognition and elevation of staff and client voices.

Theme 1: Vicarious Trauma

Across all focus groups the absorption of trauma was a recurring theme. The impact of this exposure was largely "through osmosis" (M, FG 1), where sleep would be interrupted, or a television advertisement would "set you off" (F, FG 3). While not all staff were across the term 'vicarious trauma' there was a near universal understanding of the risk factors, particularly in relation to the cumulative effects of caring work:

> "I am not sure what you do with it, because even if you tell the facts to somebody, they are not sitting in the house smelling the smells or taking in visually what you are taking in…" (F, FG 3)

> These empathetic responses range from wanting to take a small child home to "give him a bath" and to "feed him" (F, FG 2), through to the sensory manifestation of other peoples' trauma. Workers spoke about how the trauma transfers and "sits in our bodies" (F, FG 3) and how the sensory experiences associated with work seeps in:

Compassion fatigue also registered among the participants. Home life was reported to be routinely interrupted and impacted: that their families could read the situation when they walked through the door: "I don't even have to say, and these people know that I'm really not in a good place" (F, FG 1). Within the workplace the cumulative nature of the work and the need to present was well noted: "every day you go to work and try to be like, a person of hope and that in itself can get very draining" (F, FG 1).

Burnout was similarly a clear issue with a number of participants linking their sense of being overwhelmed with the feeling that they "just can't do anything about any of it" (F, FG, 3). From an organisational perspective it is worth noting that these staff members correlated that this had a direct impact upon their productivity. Moreover, this was linked to sector, organisational and/or unit expectations that underpin workload models. However, workers were clear that workload expectations cascaded down or were informed through funding models and associated key performance indicators (KPIs).

Theme 2: Workload

There are well established links between workload and burnout, something that is exacerbated for those who work with trauma. However, it is not just the amount of work but the workload imbalance (that is the increasing requirement for many 'hats' compromises the wellbeing of many workers). This reflects the need for employees to have a sense of control within the work environment.[21]

Indeed, one participant felt well-equipped to deal with serious situations where they were trained and was within their job description. Given their area of work and expertise they were able to deal with and process a client suicide. While tragic and sad, the worker understood the complexities of what they were dealing with. Workplace support was in place (but not necessarily required in this instance) as the

---

21 Wilson, F. Identifying, Preventing, and Addressing Job Burnout and Vicarious Burnout for Social Work Professionals, Journal of Evidence-Informed Social Work, 2016; 13(5), 479-483.

situation matched the worker's expectations of what might happen through the course of their work.

However, due to changing working practices and having to wear 'more hats' the person found themselves working in a palliative care-type scenario. Within this work environment they felt unprepared and found the experience to be troubling. The unfamiliarity of the situation – that is, the changed work practices – directly impacted the wellbeing of the worker. While flexibility and the ability to change is required within the workplace, consideration of expertise as they map against potential traumatic situations needs to be a consideration.

The cult of busy

Another concern that was raised across all focus groups is what we have termed the 'cult of busy'. The interiorisation of a logic around work as a primary driver in some peoples' lives was identified as a problem. This, of course, is not unique to the sector and reflects a broader issue within our society's political economy (see Louth & Potter).[22]

Participants called for well-regulated boundaries, clear lunch breaks and sustainable workloads. What was evident was the level of variation across the organisation, with some units employing strategies to better deal with workload boundaries, while others had to self-manage. Yet a common sentiment was that too many workers had bought into the cult of being busy:

> "…I know other people that book back-to-back visits, no lunch break and they kind of celebrate it and I just think

---

22 Louth, J. and Potter, M. 'The production of neoliberal subjectivities: constellations of domination and resistance', in J. Louth and M. Potter (eds.), Edges of Identity: The Production of Neoliberal Subjectivities, Chester: Chester University Press, 2017. p. 1–25.

man, a year from now you're going to be in a different industry because you just can't last like that" (F, FG 1)

"...I feel like some workers, their identity is in doing everything and working hard and not complaining ... Doing overtime and case notes on a Sunday morning. So, then you're up against that." (F, FG 2)

The quotes above illustrate two points of concern.

The first relates to how burnout is an actual workplace hazard that needs to be managed. There will always be too much work to do and if workflow is not appropriately managed it will likely impact those who work without consideration to their wellbeing. The second point is how this 'cult of busy' potentially impacts all workers. As a phenomenon, it creates a situation where workers are compared to one another with the overall completion of tasks becoming an accepted and even celebrated yardstick (that is exacerbated in magnitude over time). The potential consequence is that workloads incrementally increase and important boundaries are blurred (e.g. home and work, lunch breaks, annual leave) as more outside of workhours become normalised and accepted practice. Vitally, it is the enabling culture, not necessarily an organisation's formal workplace policies that require particular vigilance in relation to this simmering workplace issue.

Theme 3: Support

Support emerged as a central theme. The low staff turnover rate within CCFS reflects an established culture of support. However, it was clear that there is a division between formal and informal support practices. In addition, while acknowledging its importance, there was a level of cynicism towards self-care.

Formal Support

Formal support structures within CCFS are well established and were identified by participants. These structures include the Employee Assistance Program (EAP) through to clinical supervision and reflective practice. In respect to clinical supervision, it must be an empowering and collaborative process where trust and choice in a safe space allows the supervisee to disclose and reflect.[23] There was clear evidence of this within the focus groups, but it was noted that clinical supervision was not equally available to all employees. Similarly, there were feelings that services like EAP were recommended in order to push the responsibility for care and support elsewhere. One participant felt that this was equivalent to saying: "I don't want to hear it but go talk to someone else." (F, FG 2).

Self-care

Ongoing training around self-care is a fundamental requirement and is an integral element of preventative and protective practices.[24] While supervisory practices must allow for debriefing in a non-judgemental and safe space – it must also incorporate and encourage self-care.[25]

---

23 Berger, R. & Quiros, L. Supervision for trauma-informed practice. Traumatology, 2014; 20:4, pp. 296-301.

24 Wilson, F. Identifying, Preventing, and Addressing Job Burnout and Vicarious Burnout for Social Work Professionals, Journal of Evidence-Informed Social Work, 2016; 13(5), 479-483.

25 Cox, K. & Steiner, S. Preserving commitment to social work service through the prevention of vicarious trauma. Journal of Social Work Values and Ethics, 2013; 10(1), 53-60; Dombo, E. A., & Whiting Blome, W. Vicarious Trauma in Child Welfare Workers: A Study of Organizational Responses. Journal of Public Child Welfare, 2016; 0(5), 505-523; Everly, G. S., Boyle, S. H., & Lating, J. M. The effectiveness of psychological debriefing with vicarious trauma: A meta-analysis. Stress Medicine, 1999; 15, 229-233; Howlett, S. L. & Collins, A. Vicarious traumatisation: risk and resilience among crisis support volunteers in a community organisation. South African Journal of Psychology, 2014; 44(2), 180-190; Kapoulitsas, M., & Corcoran, T. Compassion fatigue and resilience: A qualitative analysis of social work practice. Qualitative Social Work, 2015; 14(1), 86-101.

Participants identified the need to practice self-care and spoke about the need to recognise 'symptoms', including 'how they were feeling about work' and of the importance of 'looking after oneself' through an episode. This is commendable behaviour that illustrates the professionalism of the workforce and CCFS's commitment to their employees.

Yet, at the same time, some participants noted that self-care could be viewed as 'tokenistic' and reflected a broader shift around personal responsibility (see Liedenberg, et al; Bober & Regehr).[26] Indeed, there was an undercurrent that self-care advice was, in some instances, being told to "just go home and take care of yourselves" (F, FG 2), with activities like 'dog walks' and 'bubble baths' being the primary suggested course of action. Not tasks, as one participant pointed out, that could be performed while at work.

Informal support

One of the primary findings that emerged from this research is how significant informal support networks were to many of the participants. Peer support is vital.[27] This research project underscored that without peer support many employees within CCFS would not have been able to continue for any significant length of time in their roles. Often this was expressed in terms of small networks of very strong relationships or the development of an informal mentoring process. One participant noted that:

---

26 Liedenberg, L., Ungar, M. & Ikeda, J. Neo-liberalism and responsibilisation in the discourse of social workers. British Journal of Social Work, 2015; 45, 1006-1021; Bober, T., & Regehr, C. Strategies for reducing secondary or vicarious trauma: Do they work? Brief Treatment and Crisis Intervention, 2006; 6(1), 1-9.

27 McFadden, P., Campbell, A. & Taylor, B. Resilience and Burnout in Child Protection Social Work: Individual and Organisational Themes from a Systematic Literature Review. British Journal of Social Work. 2014; 45(5), 1546-1563.

"Yeah, I think it's more informal support. I have a couple of workmates that I'm quite close with that I will probably talk to daily or every second day and we share – it's pretty much supervision. I don't know how I'd go without that." (F, FG, 2)

Informal support networks – and the space to have those networks – should be considered as a fundamental reason as to why the ProQOL results for CCFS were so positive. To put it bluntly: there was (and continues to be) space for workers to support one another. Yet this finding comes with an important qualification: informal support comes with risks, including the 'dumping' of traumatic material or events on other staff. As one of the workers made clear:

"I think that there is another side to that which is a bit dangerous, as well, and that is that on top of your own caseload you hear the stories of other cases, and I know for myself, I have been at points where, 'Please don't talk to me at all about anybody else because I have got enough here without hearing another story'." (F, FG 3)

This secondary trauma from other staff is a serious consideration. With increasing workloads – especially with the focus on KPIs and other outcome-based deliverables – the ability for healthy and mutually agreeable informal support networks to be sustained or even desired becomes fraught.

Theme 4: Job Satisfaction

While there is an emphasis within the literature around the adverse consequences of empathetic labour – and this must be acknowledged – there is the counterpoint that the empathetic nature of the work is one of the key elements that also makes the work so rewarding. Job satisfaction is in part tied to the empathetic abilities of staff. These are abilities that need to be celebrated within the organisation. Moreover, they reflect a unique alignment with CCFS purpose and mission and the abilities of staff and many workers' very notion of 'self'. This is the nexus between the risk and reward of undertaking a caring role within social service provision.

This was a point made repeatedly by participants: that the strength of their clients was a point of admiration for them. One participant described it "as an honour to sit and hear those stories" while just thinking "how amazing" they are. (F, FG 3). Adding to this sentiment was how the everyday work contributes to a feeling of self-worth for the employee. Noting the curious, novel and sometimes peculiar elements to their job, there is an attachment to a sense of doing good by helping clients to identify their own strengths.

The tension between the emotional risk factors and the emotional rewards of the work, is also a recurring theme in the literature (see McFadden, et al.)[28] and identifying self-worth as 'reward' links with emerging debates around vicarious resilience.

Vicarious Resilience

For the majority of the focus group participants the concept of vicarious resilience resonated. There was some unfamiliarity with the concept, but once explained there was ready agreement as to its usefulness as an expression of their own lived experience from working alongside clients. Two predominate themes emerged from

---

28 McFadden, P., Campbell, A. & Taylor, B. Resilience and Burnout in Child Protection Social Work: Individual and Organisational Themes from a Systematic Literature Review. British Journal of Social Work. 2014; 45(5), 1546-1563.

this discussion. The first was admiration for clients: "It's like if I went through even a quarter of what you went through, I wouldn't be getting up and smiling and walking into work". (F, FG 2)

The second was on the need to focus on small wins. One participant made the point that "there is a minimum amount of success you need to experience to keep working," (M, FG 1), while another reiterated this sentiment in that "it is those little wins or those stories" (F, FG 2) that keep workers going. Resilience inspires hope and small wins fuel a sense of purpose and accomplishment. Moreover, these small wins can speak to a broader agenda of utilising vicarious resilience through a celebration of staff and client voices across the organisation.

Theme 5: Structural Issues

While not an 'everyday' issue at first glance a significant point of intersection within the focus groups related to wider structural issues and the way these factors cascade down to program level. Whether in reference to changes in government, tendering of contracts, policy development, through to workplace or sector-wide cultures, there were repeated references to the tension between service provision and organisational or sector requirements to achieve specific outcomes and to fulfil KPIs.

While sympathetic of the position that management were increasingly forced to navigate, staff could readily identify these factors as directly contributing to workload stress:

> "... one of the escalations we noticed, because our programs are all connected. They are all coming up for funding in 2019 ... it looks like we will be tendering. We won't be just rolled over, so all the managers in that area are quite under stress right now, and having to get a lot of paperwork done, a lot

of evidence stuff. They want a lot from the workers so that they can make this tender strong." (F, FG 3)

The staff voice also provides an insight into future concerns. Given that system and structural factors were an overarching and prevalent theme, then – as a listening exercise – there is value in capturing staff concerns. Staff wellbeing and retention in one of the fastest growing sectors is required in order to attain those outcomes. Advocacy that connects staff wellbeing with achieving KPIs could have multi-scaler effects across macro (the sector), meso (the organisation) and micro (workers and clients) levels.

Conclusion

Our study identified a number of key protective and predictive factors for workers in traumatic environments. Correlating these findings allows for organisations to consider meaningful interventions and policy improvements aimed at protecting and empowering their workforce. This included a focus on work satisfaction and that it strongly correlates with compassion fatigue. Informal support networks were shown to be vital to the overall health of the organisation and that the 'space between' matters for workers everyday practice. The need for effective boundary setting was clear as was the elevation of small wins.

While many organisations would feel confident that they do have strategies in place that take these factors into account it is very unlikely that they are considered as a suite of interconnected issues. This means developing polices to ensure that workers empathetic reserves are not depleted, that informal networks are given the space and time to 'breathe' without becoming burdensome. The need for cultural change to resist 'the cult of busy' so that time between clients, time for lunch and time for collegiality is protected. Similarly, the boundary between work and home life needs to be vigilantly attended to. And, finally, the client voice needs to be celebrated as it is their stories that were repeatedly shown to inspire staff and provide meaning for the important work that they undertake each and every day.

5

WHOLE-OF-CULTURE SUPPORT
Introducing the Sanctuary Model for Vicarious Trauma

Robyn Miller PhD

Working in the child and family practice field means working regularly with trauma. This requires practitioners to repeatedly listen to and empathically respond to painful and disturbing stories. Few are prepared for the degree of trauma that they will be exposed to, and this places practitioners and carers at risk of being traumatised themselves; this is often referred to as 'vicarious trauma' (Pearlman and Saakvitne, 1995) or 'secondary trauma', a closely related phenomenon (Dunkley and Whelan, 2006). Recognition is needed that the achievement of a 'truly trauma- informed' service system requires no less than a 'process of reconstitution within our organisations top to bottom' (Bloom and Farragher, 2006: p. 2) and involves all stakeholders in an organisation, from coalface staff to the upper echelons of management.

Dr Sandra Bloom's work was instrumental in developing the Sanctuary Model, which attends to the group dynamics of Out of Home Care, and other service contexts, and uses trauma-informed, organisational change strategies to support better practice (Bloom, 1994; 2000; 2004). To further develop trauma-informed, relationship-based practice MacKillop Family Services (MacKillop) began implementing the Sanctuary Model in 2012. As a Sanctuary organisation, we intentionally work to create a space where the people we work with feel safe, heard and empowered to respond to the challenging trauma that faces us every day and night and to experience growth, rather than harm.

MacKillop provides a range of family support, education, disability, grief and loss and parenting programs that are delivered mostly during extended business hours on weekdays. However, as providers of out of home care to over 700 children each night, mostly in foster care, we are a 24/7 service. Our work nationally, in providing residential care and homelessness services to 160 young people in 52 different homes (with up to four young people), requires intense engagement from all parts of MacKillop. We have a duty of care to the safety and wellbeing of the young people, but also to our rostered carers who form therapeutic teams.

We have experienced the benefits and the positive impact of Sanctuary in assisting us to prevent and respond to vicarious trauma. We work hard to grow a strong culture that reflects the Sanctuary commitments and underlines our values of justice, hope, collaboration, compassion and respect. This contribution outlines MacKillop's rich journey with the Sanctuary Model and the attention to the vicarious trauma of our staff.

Context

In order to set the context, the following provides a snapshot of residential care in Australia and at MacKillop. According to The Australian Institute of Health and Welfare (AIHW), in 2018, just over 45,800 children were in out-of-home care in Australia. Of these children, 51% were in relative/kinship care,[1] 39% were in foster, and 6% were in residential care (AIHW, 2018). Over half (54%) of

---

1 See: https://www.aihw.gov.au/reports-data/health-welfare-services/child-protection/glossary/#relative

these children in out-of-home care lived in major cities and two-fifths (42%) lived in inner and outer regional areas. Children living in remote or very remote areas were twice as likely as those in major cities to be in out-of-home care. These data showed that overall, 14% of children in out-of-home care were reported as having a disability. Indigenous children living in major cities were 17 times as likely as non-Indigenous children to be in out-of-home care, while Indigenous children living in remote and very remote areas were 9 times as likely to be in out-of-home care.

The numbers of children coming into out-of-home care in Australia are simply unsustainable and reflect the serious underinvestment nationally in preventative community and family support, and for our most vulnerable families who require early intervention.

Residential care programs within non-government organisations are the most high-risk programs for the development of primary and vicarious or secondary trauma. According to WorkCover data, staff working within these programs experience the highest rates of mental stress in their Industry Classification, second only to ambulance services; and have the twelfth highest Industry Rate overall. (One hundred and four[2], the industry average has continued to increase each year from 2013-2017.)

MacKillop's experience reveals the highest number of WorkCover claims to be 'Exposure to Mental Stress Factors', with approximately 81% of reported claims coming from out-of-home-care staff. Residential care staff are uniquely at risk of mental stress due to the complex needs of their clients. These young people have generally experienced complex trauma and frequently present with mental health and behavioural difficulties such as substance abuse, suicidal and self-harming behaviours, aggression/violence, and relationship difficulties. They are at risk of abuse, crime, exploitation, accidental

---

2   WorkCover Insurance Industry Rates and Industry Claims Cost rates for 2016/17

injury and exclusion from education.

In addition to human suffering, WorkCover claims relating to mental stress are an extreme financial burden that agencies must carry, noting that government programmatic funding is startlingly inadequate on this issue.

At MacKillop we continue to embed the Sanctuary Model by training everyone in the organisation to understand trauma and its impact – both on individuals and organisations, and instil practices and rituals that 'walk our talk'. Each staff member and each young person in our care having a proactive safety plan and a self-care plan is integral to the model. Without an understanding of the systemic impact of trauma, children and young people in out-of-home care were frequently described in terms such as 'sabotaging', 'manipulative', 'resistant' – which are inherently limiting and blaming. Practitioners often felt defeated by the young person's behaviours. In the absence of a theoretical and evidence base that could help them predict, that the young person may (unsurprisingly) develop avoidant and self-destructive behaviours, given their experience of trauma, practitioners can become blaming of the young person. The trauma-informed analysis embedded within the Sanctuary Model expects that young people will struggle to trust and fight for control, often provoking rejection; as their experience is that: 'it will come anyway as adults are untrustworthy and you may as well be in control of the rejection and get it over with' (Miller 2014).

This understanding enables practitioners and carers to conceptualise this as a normal response to abnormal traumatic events, and remain stronger in their ability to remain compassionate. Instead they can name the pain that underlies the behaviour, reassure the child that they are safe now and no-one is giving up on them, call and nurture the child to growth, and reinforce constantly that they deserve better and they can treat people respectfully, learning to manage their overwhelmingly painful and angry feelings. The model is very purposeful, encouraging practitioners to be rigorous in unpacking the history and what has happened to this child, rather than what is wrong with this child, so we can be more helpful and engaging in healing responses and creative in our influence on the negative family dynamics (Miller 2014). However, care for the carers is critically important.

The retention of experienced frontline practitioners and the potential for burn-out and vicarious trauma is an ongoing issue. The prevalence of often critical and sensational media headlines, in the absence of positive media portrayal and community recognition of child and family services practitioners, can be demoralising. Similarly, the impact of public criticism by external scrutinising bodies conducting inquiries intended to hold practitioners and the system accountable, is increasingly challenging. Australian and international leaders have publicly discussed the negative impact and consequences of these issues, on the retention of frontline practitioners, which in turn impacts negatively on children and families (DHS, 2011; Munro, 2004; Scott, 2006).

The Sanctuary Model in Australia

In Philadelphia in the 1980's Sandra Bloom and her co-developers of the Sanctuary Model, Joe Federaro and Ruth Anne Ryan, questioned why many individuals and institutions in the mental health system were reluctant to change established practices of seclusion and restraint and forced medication, even though these practices were so frequently associated with negative - sometimes disastrous - outcomes for the patients and for the staff (Bloom 2010). The overall objective of the model they went on to develop is to provide an environment within which healing from traumatic experiences can occur (Esaki et al., 2013).

The Sanctuary Model came to Australia in 2008 through the Victorian Department of Human Services which was during major reform seeking better ways to look after children in residential care. In my former role with the department, I was requested to visit and review a range of models for out of home care in the UK and USA.

I recommended the Sanctuary Model be taught to our agencies in Victoria because of its awareness of 'whole of organisation approach' and the coherent understanding of trauma and vicarious trauma – its impacts on children and families, and on staff alike. As an organisational change model, it paid attention to implementation and the need to have a shared language and tools across the whole organisation, top down, bottom-up, for front-line staff and for all back of house and support staff. It was also flexible enough to 'fit' the Australian context and the range of different programs that are provided across the sector. It was sensitive to the need for cultural safety and this has since been developed and formalised through the work of our Aboriginal colleagues.

As distinct from manualised evidence-based models that require tight adherence to a particular therapeutic intervention with strict exclusion criteria, the Sanctuary Model embedded emotionally intelligent and compassionate practice with families, and care for staff as the expectation across the agency. As it is an overarching framework, it welcomes other therapeutic modalities that are complementary, for example other trauma treatment approaches such as EMDR (Eye Movement Desensitisation and Reprocessing) and TCI (Therapeutic Crisis Intervention) which we have subsequently integrated into our practice at MacKillop. In 2018, MacKillop conducted a pilot intervention aimed to increase the mental health and wellbeing of residential care workers in out-of-home care. The Safe Mind-Safe Body model was designed by Jenny Dwyer Associates in collaboration with MacKillop. It is an integrated model of early intervention which monitors stress and trauma symptoms in residential care staff and provides specialist intervention to those staff at risk of Post-Traumatic Stress Disorder (PTSD).

MacKillop has continued its Sanctuary journey following the first Certification after three years of implementation in 2015, until now. At the time of writing we have just received very positive feedback from our second certification in 2019. This has happened during a time of unprecedented growth for the organisation. Over the three years since certification, we have grown from 650 to over 1400 staff. This growth has had a significant effect on the roll out of Sanctuary and the training of staff. However, it is irrefutable that the growth and multiple transitions have been supported by our embrace of the Sanctuary Model, and indeed we have attracted good staff because we are a Sanctuary Organisation. In the first certification period of August 2012 until December 2015, around 635 staff completed the two-day initial Sanctuary Training. In the period of January 2016 to March 2019, over 890 staff completed Sanctuary training. We have also developed the Sanctuary Faculty to train external organisations, which we provide nationally.

Our evaluation of the impact of the model has been established through our partnership with Monash University. Since 2018 we have had two PhD students working with us to research different aspects of the Sanctuary Model within MacKillop.

Key aspects of the Sanctuary Model

The model is informed by four knowledge areas: the psychobiology of trauma, actively creating non-violent environments, social learning principles, and understanding complex system change (Bloom et al., 2003).

The model aims to implement an organisation-wide approach that involves creating and maintaining an environment that understands how children deal with trauma. A therapeutic community is provided to children that aims to mitigate the adverse effects of trauma.

The theoretical basis of the Sanctuary Model stems from four conceptual frameworks: Trauma Theory, Social Learning Theory, Nonviolence, and Complexity Theory (Abramovitz & Bloom, 2003).

Trauma theory is based on several decades of research describing the profound impact of stress on human development. The harm experienced through trauma is the way the individual's mind and body react to the experience, combined with how the individual's social group responds. In Social Learning Theory, the active use of the whole environment becomes the grounds for therapeutic change. The incorporation of Nonviolent Practice places attention on safety as an active aspect of organisational life. An understanding of complex adaptive systems, for both individuals as well as organisations, is provided by Complexity Theory.

The Model has been designed across four key pillars (Esaki et al., 2013).

1) that trauma can alter brain functioning and behaviour, and can affect whole systems/organisations;

2) the Safety, Emotion, Loss and Future (S.E.L.F) framework, which presents solutions to the complex problems of trauma and stress individually and organisationally;

3) Sanctuary Tools, which include community meetings, safety plans, red flag meetings, team meetings, psychoeducation and supervision/training;

4) the seven Sanctuary Commitments: nonviolence, emotional intelligence, social learning, democracy, open communication, social responsibility, growth, and change.

Individual workers and entire organisations are frequently exposed to collective trauma, for example, when tragedy strikes, as when a suicide occurs in an inpatient unit or a child dies who has been connected with child protective services. All too frequently, the response to such events is a "silencing response" and a chronically "blaming" culture which helps no one but hurts everyone involved. Every member of the organisation is affected by the events because of our fundamental group nature, our vulnerability to emotional contagion and to dynamic group effects. Trauma is collective (Bloom 2010) as Dr Judith Herman (1992) taught us, trauma fragments – individuals, families, organisations and communities – the recovery has to be through connection.

MacKillop has an ongoing commitment to building a safe relational world around each child. Our commitment to child focused/family centred practice is critical. Research that has looked at the factors that lead to change in families, consistently highlights the significance of relationships between clients and practitioners (McKeown, 2000; de Boer & Coady, 2007; Brandon et al, 2008; Trotter, 2013; Furlong, 2013). The same is true for supervisory and management relationships with middle managers modelling the appropriate exercise of authority and power and high levels of social and emotional competence. These attributes are more critical to achieving good outcomes than technical skills, procedural knowledge and compliance (Gibbs, Dwyer & Vivekananda, 2009).

However, relationship based, trauma-informed practitioners require high empathy which predisposes them to vicarious trauma. If organisations do not deal proactively with the vicarious trauma that is frequently experienced by staff, along with the individual harm and distress, the turnover and loss of experience and relationship-based practitioners reduces the likelihood of good outcomes for children and families, our core purpose. Working from first principles at MacKillop of 'do no harm', our ongoing commitment to the Sanctuary Model reflects a strengthened commitment to proactive prevention and early intervention to support staff and volunteers who are impacted by their empathic exposure to trauma.

Preventing and responding to Vicarious Trauma

Whilst the psychological and physical impact of trauma on individuals and organisations is well established, mitigating vicarious trauma is a challenge to all high-risk organisations. Approaches to mitigate psychosocial stressors typically focus on providing support for those already experiencing the effects of stress or trauma such as Employee Assistance Programs. Whilst these play a critical role, they overlook prevention and early intervention opportunities, such as those contained in the Sanctuary Model. There is evidence to suggest that organisations that mobilise internal resources such as peer support programs to support employees following a potentially traumatic event is more effective in preventing psychological-related work disability than relying on external services (Skogstad et al., 2013). The Sanctuary Model embeds this connection on a daily basis through community meetings, and building layers of support and professional development throughout MacKillop teams to promote a healthy, positive culture.

Literature in the trauma and vicarious trauma field has identified a number of factors to reduce the impact of direct and vicarious trauma (McCammon, 1996). From an organisational perspective, preventative factors include: healthy organisational work environments, training of employees, social support from colleagues and managers, and evidence based follow-up after a critical incident (Skogstad, Skorstad, Lie, Conradi, Heir, & Weisaeth, 2013).

Social support has been found to positively influence coping and adaption following trauma, improve social resources, and decrease isolation and loneliness. On-going supervision and peer support are the most beneficial forms of social support following vicarious traumatic exposure (Manning-Jones, de Terte, & Stephens, 2015). The tools in the Sanctuary Model and MacKillop's commitment to quality supervision and training on supervision skills and the principal practitioners' clinical input provide the means to action these research findings in practice.

Safety is the bedrock of the Sanctuary Model, and to create safe environments, which is the key to preventing vicarious trauma, it is necessary for us to embed a culture of critical reflection about how violence evolves within a group – and residential care is the most high-risk field of practice. A team that shares similar assumptions, goals and practices can develop a 'team mind', a way of working together smoothly and flexibly to provide a strong culture of safety within which traumatised and overwhelmed young people can explore the stormy world of the past while changing behaviour in the present. This is critical when there are at times up to 12 permanent rostered carers and other casual carers interacting with young people in residential homes.

The evidence base

Evidence supporting trauma-informed systems has developed over the past 20 years (TIP, 2014; Oral et al, 2016; Bryson, 2017) and there is promising evidence for the efficacy of such systems elsewhere to impact positively on the health of children and young people. However, this research has predominantly been conducted in the US and the UK, with a paucity of Australian research. Given the number of children and young people in Australia living in out-of-home care who have experienced severe and complex trauma due to sexual, physical and/or emotional abuse, and that these children face significant educational and health disadvantage, there is an urgent need to improve the outcomes for vulnerable Australian children.

Emotionally intelligent carers and practitioners require a commitment to self-care that is proactive rather than reactive; of note, this is an ethical imperative in itself (Norcoss and Guy, 2007; Tamura, 2012). Shaw, 2019 notes that the role of supervision as a preventative measure in vicarious supervision has been well established (Saakvitne et al., 2000; Vetere, 2012; Pack, 2014; Gil and Weinberg, 2015)

The Sanctuary Model is the only organisational framework recognised as a Promising Practice by the National Child Traumatic Stress Network (National Child Traumatic Stress Network, 2008). The Model has achieved a Scientific Rating of three (Promising Research Practice) by the California Evidence-Based Clearinghouse for Child Welfare (The California Evidence-Based Clearinghouse for Child Welfare, 2011). Jones and Loch (2015: 77) describe the adoption of the Sanctuary Model as 'achieving better congruence within service delivery, and a therapeutically responsive approach to the children and young people in MacKillop's care. This model forms a blueprint for building safer communities to assist children, families and staff heal from trauma (Verso Consulting, 2011).

Educators using Sanctuary are able to integrate it into their practice. In this way trauma theory and neuroscience shapes the way that adults understand student behaviour, develop insight into their own reactions and make informed decisions for supporting continued learning. The Sanctuary Model provides children and staff with skills for anticipating and resolving post-traumatic stress and vicarious trauma reactions (Ford and Blaustein, 2013).

A fundamental need for trauma impacted children is safety, with classrooms that address social and emotional well-being and belonging (CASEL, 2014; Sokolowski et al, 2013; Cane & Oland, 2014). Research supports the view that the whole of school environment is critical to supporting the healing processes in order to foster learning, health and wellbeing (Goss et al, 2017).

Embedding Structures

Training can run off like the proverbial 'water off a duck's back' unless the leadership is committed at every level to genuinely implementing the Model. In fact, if there is a cynical avoidance within teams, we have learnt that there is damage to the good intentions of newly trained staff who become quickly demoralised when the real-world culture is oppositional to the Sanctuary Model. We have been assertive in developing champions at every level, and openly directive, that this is the culture we want at MacKillop and that there is a collective duty of care to speak out if there is punitive practice or unprofessional behaviour. Whilst there is a clear valuing of democracy, we have been very clear about the commitment to social responsibility and to high expectations regarding safety, teamwork and professionalism.

MacKillop has self-funding Principal Practitioners who work hand in hand with co-ordinators, managers and directors across the organisation. Their role is to develop and enhance therapeutic care and provide fortnightly group reflective practice to all teams of carers (on top of the usual expectations of team meetings and individual supervision). Principal practitioners also develop training and supervision in systemic therapeutic frameworks across programs. This significant investment has been critical to supporting staff at the front line and in gaining more clinical expertise to work hand in hand with less qualified residential carers. We have also invested significantly in our learning and development team and in the way we recruit, induct and provide ongoing coaching, 'live supervision', and professional development. All of our carers are required to have as a minimum a Cert IV.

There are two backbone structures that hold the line within the agency regarding fidelity and ongoing energy to practice the Sanctuary Model: these are the core team and the local practice teams.

Core Team

The Core Team which has existed since 2012 currently comprises 24 members. The Core Team, which includes members from all three States in which MacKillop operates, meets face-to-face every two months from 10am-3pm and every other month by phone for one hour. The members are responsible to act as leaders and champions and to develop the agencies commitment to being trauma responsive and competent.

Local Practice Teams

Local Implementation Teams (LITs) were established in the second year of implementation. After the certification at the end of 2015, we changed the name and the focus of these team to Local Practice Teams (LPTs). This was particularly in recognition of the focus on embedding the Sanctuary Model in the three years to follow.

The LPT's are geographically distributed across MacKillop's wide reach around three states of Australia. There are currently eight Local Practice Teams across Australia and work health and safety is always on the agenda.

Conclusion: From Trauma to Growth

Whilst reducing the impact of exposure to trauma in the workplace is essential, organisations can go further. Positive responses to trauma in the workplace such as those resonating in the Sanctuary Model, can have a positive effect on employees. Qualitatively, employees often note the positive impact of their work on themselves, and the privilege of working with those who are recovering from the impact of trauma.

In a systemic review by Manning-Jones, de Terte, & Stephens (2015), a number of factors were found to have a positive relationship with post-traumatic growth:

- empathetic engagement with clients;
- optimism and positive affect;
- witnessing post-traumatic growth in direct trauma survivors;
- sense of satisfaction, competence, and value in one's work;
- engaging in self-care activities; and
- social support, in particular, supervision and peer support.

Optimising these factors through the structure and practices of Sanctuary in the workplace will buffer employees against the effects of exposure to trauma and also give them the opportunity to experience growth and enhanced wellbeing. At MacKillop our workforce engagement survey results have positively increased and our return to work rates of staff who have been impacted by trauma has improved dramatically.

6

STAFF AT THE HEART
Practical Strategies for Everyday Spiritual Support

Netty Horton and Nick Collins

Working in the human services area can be both challenging and rewarding. More often than not it is the challenging personal experiences that leave an indelible impact on us both personally and professionally. Most likely, each of us who have worked in the area of service provision can recall experiences and situations where we have been professionally challenged, emotionally impacted or even traumatised by the experiences and personal circumstances of individuals, couples and families seeking our services. While the vicarious impact of the work is to be expected to some extent this is often mitigated by good supervision, professional support and our own personal spirituality.

As social service providers it is essential that we are mindful of the conditions and cumulative impact of client related work on our understanding of issues and client presentations. As such our organisations should provide employee assistance supports and identify policies and frameworks to look after and protect staff to the best of our ability. It is critical that managers and administrators of services have a sound understanding of human services work, and the complexity and impact of this work on staff so as to manage the risk of staff being detrimentally impacted.

Often in addition to good supervision, human services staff may need time to find perspective and, in some cases, take a break from working with complex or traumatised clients - below is my own personal account.

For a while in my counselling career I counselled children and quite a fair proportion of these children had been sexually abused. While I realised that I was seeing only a small subset of a troubled population of children, (and not all children were struggling with such abuse), my experience nonetheless affected me profoundly.

As a probationary psychologist I remember one case where I was counselling a child who was found in an abandoned toilet block after her parents overdosed on heroin. Of course, this incident contributed greatly to my realisation that she didn't have a normal happy family. At the age of five she had a very real and deep understanding of drug abuse. At certain times in my work I often wonder how this particular girl (who would now be an adult) is going. I hope that she has successfully managed all the personal challenges and circumstances in her life.

Interactions such as these have a significant impact on one's professional and personal life. At that time I was a young father and the impact of these cases led me to taking a break from this particular type of case work.

It is sometimes a cliché in management literature, but it is true to say, that staff are literally at the heart of what we do, and enable us to live and express the mission of our work. At CatholicCare we do this with clients, communities and our colleagues and stakeholders. In order to do our work well we need to support and care for our workforce and demonstrate congruence between the words and actions in our support and management of staff. Good people management is a real skill and needs to be demonstrated and experienced.

In practical terms this means that we need to live the values of our organisation, and have honest true conversations, both in good times and bad. We need to be able to provide support, good supervision and training with learning pathways for staff development. We need to provide a culture that is supportive, challenging and open to learning. Also we need to respect each person's professional style and approach. We also need to encourage people to reach their potential and embrace opportunity which may mean leaving the organisation to move on to another organisation within the sector.

Challenges and uniqueness of the sector

Social service organisations need people who are willing to take up new challenges within the sector, particularly in this current climate of change and reform; for example, around the significant impact of compliance and data recording on our work. As organisational leaders managing expectations (that staff need to administer and report on programs) can be a juggle but, we also need to look to ensure that staff find their work meaningful, are connected to the organisation and the mission of the organisation and that they feel valued in their work. This requires dedicated focus and a deliberate strategy to engage and connect leaders, staff and volunteers across all levels of the organisation and programs and services. In this context we all need to be approachable, available, and promote and engage in consultation.

A key part of our work in 2020 is managing work expectation. As mentioned previously, the demands and context of work is changing and we have a unique ability to provide leadership in a way that is very different to other sectors, to lead through this change having a strong alignment between our values, our mission and our social justice mandate. In caring for our staff, it is critical to provide the culture and place where people can be their best self in their work –

where they can also be true to their spiritual values and practices that help them in sustaining their commitment to the work they do. Good leadership can drive this workplace culture.

Organisational culture and spirituality

Building an open and transparent work place culture where staff are valued and recognised is paramount to organisational success. Staff surveys, representation on committees, regular newsletters, CEO updates, emails from team leaders, regular consultation and staff meetings with groups of staff, having a curious and inquisitive approach to service delivery and actively striving to hear the voice of the client or family at any time, all contribute to a positive workplace culture.

This strong sense of recognition is important, and can be achieved through a range of activities. Activities such as team building that consolidate a culture of respect and demonstrate a willingness by management and the leadership team to listen and learn from their staff experience. Other activities include celebrating milestones, acknowledgements of service and morning tea gatherings.

Issues and Concerns of Staff

At CatholicCare our focus is providing services and addressing need, as such, it is imperative to the success of our programs that we be attuned to the everyday challenges and issues of our staff so that they are enabled to respond to the needs of our clients.

As leaders and providers in social services we need to keep ourselves grounded in the reality of the work we do, seek honest feedback and be flexible in our thinking to allow us to review and reset what we do based on new information or new evidence and have integrity to do what is right even if it is very difficult.

While client- facing work and responding to need is the foundation of what we do, the environment in which we work is changing and becoming more challenging. Increasingly there are more demands on workers' time to respond to compliance and risk requirements, more data entry to record service activity and increasing resources required to manage time and service productivity.

In the main these are reasonable and necessary requirements to ensure the effective and efficient use of resources and public funds for services. Better data recording across the service system ensures that there is an emerging body of evidence to inform service productivity, clinical effectiveness, resource decision making and demand and service drivers.

These types of metrics are being used to measure performance, however at the same time we need to support staff, who have significant workplace demands upon them, to understand and deal with the change across the sector, and organisationally, and what it means. If we empower staff to improve our collective culture and help inform the agenda, this sends a powerful message to them that the work they do is critical to clients but also serves as an advocacy agenda to improve the service system with which they work.

As leaders we need to provide feedback to staff on the various reasons and need for data collection, provide evidence of the trends and issues for clients from the data we collect, and help staff see the benefits and need for good data entry and data integrity. This serves a purpose over and above compliance and contractual requirements. Specifically we, as service professionals, have a duty and obligation to:

- provide feedback to government regarding policy and how policy and programs are impacting our clients – (via advocacy and awareness raising); and

- create or maintain a safety net or support for the most marginalised in our community as evidenced by our data and experience as service providers.

If we don't do this we are providing a disservice to our clients and staff and we are not realising and providing the care to support and change systems. Many individuals and staff in the social services sector enter it to 'make a difference', 'work with people', 'address and advocate for disadvantage and social justice'.

In the current environment these motives are sometimes hard to realise as we see the increasing regulatory burden on services.

Good clinical oversight and intense work and connection with clients is not the only data metric we need to monitor. We also need to capture emerging evidence to support better service delivery.

As leaders it is critical to organisational success and a healthy workforce that we seek to understand the challenges we are all confronted with in our roles. By living the values of our organisation with our staff, we can support and nurture a culture of caring.

As we reflect on our personal and professional lives it is often the tough times we remember most. We are constantly challenged to grow and learn, and it is true we seem to learn more from our failures than our successes.

Having the capacity to reflect on our own behaviour and learn from our collective experiences helps to provide the opportunities for our staff and volunteers to do the same. This reflection helps us to deal with conflicting priorities and values, balancing the needs of our staff and our volunteers, with the dignity, demands and needs of our clients.

This isn't always easy. There are times when staff express feelings of vulnerability and anxiety in responding to people who they perceive as aggressive or threatening. Non-clinical advice might include building physical barriers, glass screens, locking doors or even, on occasions, engaging security staff. While everyone has the right to feel safe in the workplace, such responses can severely traumatise our clients. Instead, taking a clinical approach, it is possible to implement positive and effective measures to assist clients to manage their behaviour. At the same time, it is, equally important to provide training for staff and volunteers to understand trauma, so they can respond appropriately to a range of different encounters.

There may also be times when staff are facing personal or professional challenges which impact on their ability to work with clients. It is through clinical supervision that we may identify when the staff challenges are impacting on how they support their clients.

It is vital in our organisations that we build workplaces that are flexible, and that acknowledge the potential impact of vicarious trauma on staff within our human resources practices.

Impact of change and reform on the sector

Our sector is one that has been subject to significant and systemic change. Competitive tendering, the emphasis on financial viability, changing policy priorities and funding arrangements, and the priority of consumer directed care all shape the responses of our agencies and our workforce.

The impact of COVID-19 has highlighted how adaptable and nimble we need to be as leaders to support the people who deliver the services on the front line.

Transparency, authenticity, and treating people with dignity are all critical considerations in ensuring our treatment and work practices are consistent with our values. In the Catholic social service sector we value the principles of Catholic Social Teaching and working for the common good.

At Catholic Care our mission and values reflect a compassionate and caring approach. We seek to serve to provide the best quality of services that we can in an inclusive and non-judgemental environment. We can only continue to do this work by investing in our people, by recognising their contribution to our work, by providing them with the supports they require to maintain their strength and resilience, and most of all in valuing them as individuals. We can do this because of the nature of our organisation and because we understand the value of caring for those who care in ensuring our commitment to those seeking our support.

In this current climate of COVID-19 we have learned many lessons. We have had to rise to the challenge to understand a quickly changing social landscape and consider the predictions of what might be the 'new normal'. The level of trauma associated with the pandemic, social isolation, stress and family violence is becoming more evident. To work effectively in this environment and to ensure the wellbeing and safety of our staff and clients we have invested in clear and timely communication to all staff both within the leadership team and to experts delivering services on the frontline. Because of strong communication combined with the expertise of our staff and support of our volunteers we have been able to adapt our service models and responses to this new and evolving environment – always with the view of ensuring best practice work environment for our staff.

7

WALKING THE WALK

Leading Catholic Organisations that Foster Connection

Belinda Clarke and Kylie Burgess

Positive human connections are at the heart of the mission of Catholic ministries. This central characteristic of ministry reflects the grounding Catholic theological perspective that "relationships" enable "the process of becoming human"[1]. Understanding the sacredness of relationships is a foundational principle guiding how Catholic social services operate: from health to social work and counselling to housing, children's services, disability and aged care. It follows that staff and the organisational culture within Catholic social services are appropriately supported and nurtured to enable and facilitate healthy human connections, both internally, with one another, and externally, with the people we serve. Hosting and holding environments that ensure our social services ministries and the people who serve in them, including the leaders, are sustained and healed within a contemporary setting is critical. This contribution examines different aspects of this responsibility and explores learnings that may add value to existing structures, gathered from a 2000-year tradition of ministry, spirituality and supporting positive human connections.

---

1 Selling, J. A. Reframing Catholic Theological Ethics. Oxford: Oxford University Press; 2016.

This contribution does not seek to provide answers. Our intent is to start a conversation and invite reflection on the following questions:

- What specific responsibilities do we as leaders of Catholic social services, have to enable a culture and provide systems that are human centred and proactively support teams engaged in relational ministries?

- How does our organisation provide space and opportunity for staff to be nurtured so that they can sustain positive human connections, particularly when they are engaged in challenging professional relationships and during seasons of personal and professional struggle?

- What can the Catholic tradition offer us to assist in this responsibility?

- How can Jesus' ministry inform the way we operate?

- Where do we look to draw inspiration and learnings from the stories and experiences of founders of ministries, community leaders and the communion of saints?

Caring in Context

The South Australian Study in this book uncovered a not too surprising fact that the negative impact on staff who are immersed in the suffering of others on a daily basis requires "immediate attention" to ensure burnout does not deplete the workforce[2]. This research is evidence that people involved in frontline service ministries need to be effectively cared for and nurtured. Furthermore, where the work involves relationships with people experiencing suffering and trauma,

---

2   Louth,J., Mackay, T., Karpetis, G. & Goodwin-Smith, I. Understanding Vicarious Trauma. 2019. http://centacare.org.au/wp-content/uploads/corporate/VicariousTraumaReport.pdf

such as many of the mission driven Catholic social service ministries, the challenge to avoid burnout and support staff appropriately is amplified. Many people, including leaders in the "helping" professions of Catholic social services are tired, and for good reason, the "continual use of empathy and concern for others is enormously draining"[3]. Leaders of Catholic social services continue to be called to reflect on what can be done to support staff and the organisation to limit the impact of burnout.

There has been significant and varied research to demonstrate that "spiritual beliefs and practices can reduce the effects of burnout on social workers"[4]. A literature review on the spirituality of mental health professionals found that experienced therapists reported that personal practices of spirituality were essential to their mental health and emotional wellbeing. Posluns and Gall found that spiritual practices including mindfulness; meaning making in work; prayer and spending time in nature[5] supported health and wellbeing in practitioners. Human service professionals are increasingly looking to spiritual practices to support their clients to connect, belong and make meaning. Our personal experience as leaders in social services and other ministries is that an understanding of spirituality as part of integral human development and wellbeing is beneficial to individuals, organisations and ultimately to the people we serve.

Franciscan nun and theologian Ilia Delio defines tradition as

---

3   Siebert, D & Siebert, C, The Caregiver Role Identity Scale: A Validation Study Research on Social Work Practice. 2005; 15 (3), p. 204-212
4   Godoy, A. & Allen, N., "Does Spirituality reduce the effects of burnout?". Electronic Theses, Projects, and Dissertations. 478. 2017. https://scholarworks.lib.csusb.edu/etd/478
5   Posluns, K. and Gall, T. Dear Mental Health Practitioners Take Care of Yourselves. International Journal for the Advancement of Counselling. 2019. P 1-20. https://www.semanticscholar.org/paper/Dear-Mental-Health-Practitioners%2C-Take-Care-of-a-on-Posluns-Gall/1b745fed637dce72e67a6ae0ad6ba0ddc88300c9 (accessed 29/9/2019)

the continual presence of a particular spirit that assimilates the past into the present, enabling the values and ideas to continue to serve the present[6]. The history of Catholic social service agencies is positioned within the larger Catholic tradition. This tradition constitutes an identity which becomes a resource to meet present and future demands on these agencies as they realize the mission of Jesus in the world. For CatholicCare Tasmanian staff, The Archbishop's Charter articulates this reality, stating that "CatholicCare Tasmania stands in the long tradition of Catholic service to those in need. It seeks above all to enhance the human life of people by offering the full Christian vision for human life. This is its particular identity and its special mission"[7].The Catholic identity of social service agencies is expressed through certain characteristics, for example a belief in the dignity of the person, an emphasis on sacramental relationships and a preferential option for the poor[8]. Whole-of-person care is at the heart of the Catholic tradition. This not only situates the focus of our efforts towards the people we serve, but also those who work in our agencies.

In seeking to develop the nurturing environments required to foster positive human connections, leaders of Catholic social services have a unique opportunity to lean into and reflect on the wealth of experience within the Catholic tradition to draw inspiration, particularly in relation to spirituality and service. Before Catholic social services was an "industry" or "profession" the people involved in comparable ministries and services often belonged to voluntary communities and religious orders. Were there healthy practices in

---

6   Delio, I. The Future of Tradition. 2019. https://omegacenter.info/the-future-of-tradition/(accessed 20/9/2019)

7   Archbishop Julian Porteous DD. The Archbishops Charter, CatholicCare Tasmania. 2019.

8   O'Connell, L. and Shea, J. Tradition on the Move, Leadership Formation in Catholic Health Care. MLC Press: Sacramento; 2013. P 45.

place to help members of these communities sustain their vocations that we can learn from? How did these people support one another? How did they make sure they did not burnout?

Despite the wisdom that exists within the Catholic tradition, reflection on this learning is incredibly challenging and complex at the moment. There is sadness and shame in and around the Catholic Church including within social services. The Church continues to undergo significant and appropriate scrutiny, particularly in relation to institutional and personal abuse of power, sexual abuse and the misuse of relationships. So we go cautiously, with open eyes. The learnings from the recent uncovering of abuse can and must help reshape the future of our Church, in particular our understanding of human relationships and power. The responses required are many and varied. They have begun with the Church taking responsibility for and repairing, where possible and appropriate, damaged and broken relationships and people. There is also a need to support leaders across the Church, including lay leaders of Catholic organisations, such as social services, to lead with a renewed understanding that sacred human connections are the essence of the ministries they steward. This requires authenticity, vulnerability and strength. As we learn from enormous past errors, we can also be intentional about celebrating the wealth of positivity and green shoots of life that are not enmeshed in the deep failings.

The current context of Catholic social services is undeniably complex. Individuals and organisations are grappling with Catholic identity and delivery, mission and margin, funding options and contracts, staff support and expectations, and seemingly increasing client complexity and suffering. Continuing to deliver mission driven services which honour the human dimension and the sacred relationship between people within a competitive environment is hard. There is a critical risk that the very components that require successful human connections to succeed will be diminished through a range of organisational and contextual changes and shifting priorities. Catholic social services must determine and develop innovative strategies to enable them to advance mission in the current context. "Mission verses margin" discussions occur at many decision-making tables in Catholic organisations, and while this dialogue is useful, it is not always beneficial to see mission and margin as competing forces. Strong financial stewardship, social entrepreneurship and commercial acumen are effective and demonstrated approaches to support Catholic social services to continue to operate and deliver exceptional mission driven care and support. The important component is ensuring that as organisations discern a way forward in this complex environment, they seek a gospel inspired strategy and shared understanding of who they serve, why they do what they do, how they make a difference and how changes to service delivery continue to align to mission.

A Social Impact approach

At CatholicCare Tasmania, we developed a social impact approach and framework, which draws on a Catholic theological worldview to articulate a person-centred integrated approach to strengthening individual, family and community wellbeing. In the Framework, there are seven social impact domains: health, education, housing, safety, community engagement, economics and spirituality. These domains express the Catholic teaching that authentic human development concerns every dimension of the whole person and the community in which they live[9].

Following the implementation of our social impact framework people experiencing spiritual wellbeing:

1. experience meaning, hope and purpose through a sense

---

9   https://catholicecology.net/blog/pope-francis-what-integral-human-development

of connection to something other than themselves (for example a faith tradition);

2. have positive, trusting relationships and a sense of belonging; and

3. are free and able to express their cultural, religious, and spiritual practices.[10]

This articulation of the role of spirituality in wellbeing can also be applied to how Catholic human service organisations view the spiritual wellbeing of staff. It provides a basis for us to proactively evaluate how our organisations foster meaning, hope, purpose and connection for staff and clients. Do we intentionally cultivate positive, trusting relationships and a sense of belonging across our teams? How do we offer opportunities for our people to safely express their diverse cultural, religious and spiritual practices? Asking critical questions such as these can assist us to pinpoint areas to focus efforts to create healthy and nurturing environments where human connections flourish.

Intrinsic to the call to leadership of Catholic organisations is the call to host spaces of hope and healing. This includes being attentive to organisational dysfunction that could be contributing to the prevalence of burnout. Doohan (2011, p81) suggests that "leaders who want to have a healing effect on an organisation must listen to workers' stories and anger, call them to community, health and wellness"[11]. This includes stopping negative influences and destructive practices from within the organisation itself. Capacity to lead in this way takes courage and a capacity to deal with our own pain

---

10 Clarke, B & Burgess K. Social Impact Program Framework. 2019. www.hobartsip.org

11 Doohan, L. (2011). Courageous Hope, The Call of Leadership. Paulist Press: New York; 2011.

and the pain of others'[12].

In reflecting and reviewing the positive learnings and inspirations within the Catholic tradition, there needs to be careful consideration into how we share and use these learnings to inform current practices and strategies. Practices developed within religious orders and for Catholic communities in the past were done for people who, in the main were devout Catholics. In contrast, current leaders and ministers of Catholic social services are not united in a shared faith or set of beliefs. The spirituality, faith and meaning making practices of people leading and working in Catholic social services is incredibly diverse. Many of us are not Catholic, Christian or adherents of a faith tradition. However, we are all united in our shared work with the Catholic Church. The question for us is not only how to connect people to relevant and meaningful aspects of the Catholic tradition but how to do this in a manner that is inclusive, affirming and nurturing. If we do not get this part right, if how we do this excludes people, or if it leads to judgement, then we demonstrate a lack of understanding of the human person, relationships and respect, and risk doing further damage. The Catholic tradition that we bring forward into the present and future needs to embody its theological worldview through fostering and supporting an environment of belonging, trust and positive relationships.

Bringing forward the Catholic tradition

The retelling and contextualising of foundation stories of humble and heroic leadership can offer inspiration to staff engaged in the diverse works of Catholic social services. Inspiration comes from Venerable Catherine McAuley, St Marcellin Champagnat, Venerable Mary Potter, St Mary Mackillop, Venerable Nano Nagle, Catherine

---

12   Ibid p 85

De Hueck Doherty and Fr John Wallis. These people were inspired to respond in a specific way, in their time and place to a personal experience of God, Jesus and the Holy Spirit. The responses are incredibly diverse and powerful; from street nursing and care, teaching and supporting children with no home or family, caring for women who are abandoned and people who live diminished lives. These founders, and many of their followers have supported, cared, educated, housed and loved millions of people, particularly people who experience vulnerabilities and suffering. Our Catholic tradition (continued in Catholic social services) is a proud home to countless inspirational leaders and people who have lived committed lives of relentless positive regard for all. We need to tell and retell the stories.

A good way to support and connect people through the Catholic tradition is to share real stories. Talking with staff about Mother Teresa, who she was, her vision, her human fears and concerns, and her love of people living in the streets of Calcutta can lead to fantastic conversations about how we can learn and follow her example in how we care for people and how we can connect with the people we serve. Sharing the story of St Maximilian Kolbe who volunteered to die in place of a stranger in the death camp Auschwitz, and the real impact of this sacrifice on the "stranger" who went on to live a life of service, can support staff to tap into their own motivations for working in Catholic social services. There is a communion of saints and leaders that we can look to as exemplars, as guides and companions to inform how we develop and hold healthy and healing relationships and environments.

As a Catholic community we are also primarily called to reflect deeply on our original founding story. Catholic organisations are enlivened through exploring and articulating how and what Jesus' life, death and resurrection means for people and organisations continuing the vast ministries this story has sparked and sustained.

Across Australia many Catholic communities and ministries are grappling with how to enable the Catholic tradition to continue to guide and serve contemporary practice and culture. There are also many creative and effective responses that we can look to for inspiration. Whole-of-person care is a foundational concern in Catholic Health Australia and Catholic Social Services Australia sponsored Ministry Leadership Program[13]. In one specific session of the program, leaders are presented with a model of support and burnout and are encouraged to reflect on their own experience. This practice of individual reflection within a supportive community of leaders encourages leaders to revisit and draw from their own journey through similar situations and consider how the organisation might respond to compassion fatigue. It would be wonderful to learn from all the practices and initiatives from across Catholic social services and beyond that are nourishing human connections and supporting environments of hope and healing.

Many Catholic inspired ministries, including religious orders and parishes demonstrate an extensive and deep understanding of vocation and have developed tools, rituals and spiritual practices to support people seeking to work, minister and live in a vocational manner. These diverse practices, supports and rituals inform how we continue to nurture healthy and healing environments within a Catholic context.

What does it look like to be organisations that offer staff spaces to draw on Catholic spirituality to sustain and strengthen their call to the work? Below are two different specific examples.

---

13 O'Connell, L. and Shea, J. Tradition on the Move, Leadership Formation in Catholic Health Care. MLC Press: Sacramento; 2013. P 157.

Reassessing vocation during a season of burnout

A leader in a Catholic social service organisation experienced a season of physical and emotional burnout. The organisation was going through significant restructure, a major program was causing stress and they were facing a family crisis. The leader, at the end of their resources, stepped away from the job which was a core expression of their sense of ministry and identity.

This leader, while not identifying as a Catholic, had been introduced to Ignatian spirituality and during the season of recovery committed to a program of Spiritual Exercises In Daily Life facilitated by Kardia Formation.[14] The retreat involves a daily commitment of 60-90 minutes in prayer and reflection centred on the themes of the life of Christ using poetry, scripture and music as prompts for deep reflection. The leader met weekly with the spiritual director for over nine months. This leader reflects:

"This rich tradition drawn from St Ignatius' life work, saved my life. Being accompanied through the disorder of burnout and its impact on everything, my confidence and self-worth, my identity, my spirituality, supported me to come through the season restored and more deeply acquainted with who I am and my calling to the work of Catholic mission in its social services. After several months I was able to find fresh energy and vision and a new role in a different context but still within a Catholic ministry."

Anon.

---

14 See: http://www.kardia.com.au/about/kardia-directors/

Making Catholic Identity accessible and relatable to staff – A personal account

In 2017, in my role as Director of Mission with CSSA, I worked with the Mission Engagement Officer at a CatholicCare agency to run a series of six workshops on Catholic Social Teaching. Most of the staff involved did not identify as Catholic, Christian or having any faith.

The purpose of these workshops was to be a place where staff could:

- Explore the connection between CatholicCare's mission and identity, their personal values, sense of meaning, purpose and vocation;
- Learn more about Catholic Social Teaching and how it applies to the work of CatholicCare; and
- Further integrate the sense of mission and identity and Catholic Social Teaching into their day to day work.

The first workshop intentionally gave opportunity for each individual to reflect on their own values and what motivates them in their lives and their work. Discussion focused on where they sat on a spectrum of respect to resonate with organisational values and tangible ways that they each saw them expressing these values through their work.

Feedback from participants included comments that they had not seen the values of the organisation in this way, as life giving and energising for their work. Several commented that they wanted to know more about the Catholic tradition as while they did not identify, they felt how their worldview resonated and this gave them a fresh energy for the work they were doing and the challenges they were facing.

Kylie Burgess

These accounts are but two examples of ways to make Catholic spirituality accessible for staff. Others include:

- provide board, leadership and staff formation that includes a focus on meaning making, vocation and service;

- familiarise staff with the key elements of the Catholic Church's social doctrine as outlined in the Compendium of Social Teaching and work through how these elements relate to their daily work and practice;

- use Church teachings such as Catholic Social Teaching to inform service models. This can be done through asking key questions when we are designing programs;

- ensure all policies, procedures and systems support human dignity and connection;

- facilitate individual and team prayer, reflection and meditation;

- use scripture stories such as The Road to Emmaus and the parable of The Good Samaritan to inspire action and help discernment;

- use current papal teachings such as Laudato Si as a way for staff to connect to current issues of social concern;

- support people through connection to spiritual accompaniment, also known as spiritual direction, alongside other forms of supervision;

- provide access to and participation in the sacraments; and

- connect people to the broader Church community.

The Catholic tradition and the people who have lived and worked within it, in the past and the present contain an abundance of understandings about the human condition, relationships and connections with one another as well as with our environments. These need to continue to inform how we engage with the diversity of people in our spheres of influence in order to help us "serve the present".

Conclusion

Our contribution began with an invitation to reflect on our experience. Margaret Mary Flynn IBVM, founding director of CatholicCare Wilcannia-Forbes and previous leader of the Australian and South East Asian province of the Loreto Sisters, insisted that to sustain our leadership we need to take time out to reflect on our experience and become reacquainted with our deeper inspiration[1]. This personal spiritual practice becomes the well from which leaders are able to create opportunities for staff and communities to do the same. We conclude with this insight in the hope of supporting leaders who seek to walk the walk and lead organisations that are places of deep and personal human connection and love.

---

1   Flynn, M. The Heart of the Matter, in Listening, Learning and Leading: The impact of Catholic identity and mission. McMullen, G. & Warhurst J. (Eds.) Connor Court Publishing: Ballarat; 2014. P 22.

CONCLUSION

Jesus (Mark 6:7-13) instructs his disciples to teach, heal and be present – and this is what we strive to do in our work within Catholic social services – we teach, we heal and as social service workers, we seek to be fully present so that we may help those who are struggling and in need.

The Gospels are replete with examples of healing; healing involves wellness while acknowledging mind body and spirit[2]. And in reading these essays I have reflected on how these teachings might be reflected within our workplace cultures.

It is obvious to me that mere administration of business and compliance with human resource practices, while critical and not to be diminished, are not enough to sustain us in the social services sector – what will give us strength and provide the avenue for restoration is our spirituality.

Spirituality gives meaning to us as individuals, and as such shapes our organisations and our sector. I believe our spirituality can help us to find meaning, comfort and hope. Spirituality is idiosyncratic, it is individual, and it is personal – we come to it differently – but ultimately it makes us richer, soothes us and has the capacity to calm our worried mind.

In the year that I have headed up Catholic Social Services Australia I have visited many of our member organisations, spoken with leaders as well as practitioners who work on the frontline. I see how leaders and colleagues work together, and I see how effective leadership,

---

2 https://www.chausa.org/publications/health-progress/article/may-june-2018/chaplains-pope-francis-and-the-healing-encounter

organisational strategy and culture provide the means to build a strong workforce. I see how these leaders have shaped organisational strategy, and the culture and values imbued within them provide the opportunity for a clear and robust pathway forward to enable us to nourish our social service sector organisations and individuals working within.

But also, I feel, not only see. I feel the culture of caring when I physically walk into many of our member organisations. I feel the respect and recognition of colleagues to each other, of human services workers to clients and leaders to those whom they lead. I feel it through actions, words of kindness, displays of kindness, compassion and patience towards people often gravely in need – ultimately I feel the respect for the dignity of the human – and for all that is human within each and every one of us.

I hope these essays have been informative, that they may have given meaning to current work you may be doing or that they have raised questions as to how you might deal with issues differently – but above all I hope that they lift you to consider the soulfulness of how we work and how we administer that work – in a modern contemporary social services sector.

In closing we have included below some questions for reflection that might assist in creating conversations about spirituality, leadership and a caring workforce.

Dr Ursula Stephens,

CEO Catholic Social Services Australia

Questions for Reflection

- How do you give yourself time to engage with your spirituality – how does it provide meaning, comfort and hope to you as an individual?

- Reflect on a time when it was your faith and/or spiritual practices that sustained, rescued or renewed you.

- Share a story that encapsulates and embraces the realities of inclusive love, enduring hope, virtuous life or sustaining faith.

- How might Indigenous cultural practice and governance help non-Indigenous organisations to approach leadership differently and provide alternative solutions for problems encountered in the social services workforce?

- What have you learned from these contributions that your leadership team can learn from to strengthen genuine and deep human connection within your services?

- How can the approaches discussed within this book, such as the Sanctuary Model, assist with developing a workplace culture that has an inherent understanding of trauma and vicarious trauma and its impacts on children, families and staff alike?

- Explore the impact of gender, culture and experience on your work and leadership in the social service sector.